VEGAN
Simplicity

VOLUME ONE

Many Blessings!

Chef Mark Anthony

D1444949

ISBN-13: 978-0-9828791-0-8
ISBN-10: 0-9828791-0-5

Printed in the United States of America

Cover and Text Design: Holmes Printing Solutions
Back Cover Photos: Nicole Issa-Warren

To order books, request information or comment contact:
Mark Anthony M.A.L.L.
Box 332
Ashland, KY 41105-0332
E-mail: spicecreator@yahoo.com

Holmes Printing
solutions LLC

8757 County Road 77
Fredericksburg, OH 44627
888.473.6870

Table of Contents

Fun Recipes From The Vault

I hope you have as much fun with these recipes as I have had making this collection. As with all cooking, use your creative senses and go beyond the limitations of any recipe. I have always thought of recipes as a guide. You can always make substitutions, add something different, or even prepare it different. Make every recipe your own signature.

If you want to create a very special holiday gift for someone, try this. Take all your favorite recipes and print them up on some nice paper or card stock. Do some really fancy packaging on it or even make an index box. It would be something so special to give and something so special to receive. I can't think of a better gift than your own very personal secret family recipes given to your best friend. To me, that is the purpose of recipes, to share them.

When I was growing up my mother did not use too many recipes; only for baking and some sauces. I was trained by a lot of old school chefs that never used a recipe. We would cook in batches for hundreds, and the food would turn out the same every time. I have probably thousands of recipes in my vault. Some were given to me; others were from restaurants I managed and owned over the years past. I get many today emailed to me. Most of them, I have put on my own twist and a couple are great just the way they are and I haven't changed a thing.

Vegan cooking is a fun and exciting challenge. Today, there is a vegan substitute for almost everything. The one thing you want to be aware of is that a lot of these items have more chemicals and preservatives than the regular processed foods you are substituting them for. I strongly suggest reading the labels and whenever possible; use only fresh natural foods.

I have been cooking my entire life and I still find new and fun things to do. I am always learning and looking for something different. There is always more to learn. God has gifted us with that desire and He never runs out of new ideas and discoveries for us to experience.

Thank you for your interest in this and other books. I encourage you to jump right in and have fun. You can also check out my fun website at www.ChefMarkAnthony.com. Email me; I would love to hear from you.

Be Blessed,

Mark Anthony

APPETIZERS & DRINKS

....................Tomato Bruschetta.....

Eight Layer Fiesta Dip

2 avocados, and diced
2 Tbsp. lemon juice
⅛ tsp. salt
1 recipe *Black Bean Dip*
1 cup *Cilantro Tofu Sour Cream*
1 cup *Sunshine Salsa*
1 cup vegan shredded cheddar
1 - 4 oz. can diced green chilies
½ cup black olives, sliced
½ cup green onion, thinly sliced
tortilla chips

In a small glass bowl, combine the avocados, lemon juice, and salt, mash until smooth with a fork, and set aside. On a large platter, baking pan, or bowl, place the *Black Bean Dip* and spread to a smooth and even layer. Evenly spread the mashed avocados over the bean dip, followed by the *Cilantro-Tofu Cream* and *Sunshine Salsa*, and then sprinkle the remaining ingredients over the top. Cover & chill for several hours. Serve with tortilla chips.

Serves 10-12

Cilantro Tofu Sour Cream

12 oz tofu, firm
¼ cup freshly chopped cilantro
⅓ cup soy milk
3 Tbsp. lemon juice
1 Tbsp. nutritional yeast
½ tsp. salt

In a food processor, blend all of the ingredients until smooth. Transfer mixture to a glass bowl. Cover and chill for 1 hour. Serve just as you would use sour cream.
Yield: 2 ½ cups

Black Bean Dip

⅓ cup green onion, thinly sliced
1 tsp. garlic, minced
1 Tbsp. olive oil
1 tsp. cumin
1 - 15 oz. can black beans, drained and rinsed
½ cup water
¼ cup freshly chopped cilantro
2 Tbsp. lime juice
1 tsp. chipotle chilies juice or puree
½ tsp. salt

In a small skillet, sauté the green onions and garlic in olive oil for 3-4 minutes or until softened. Add the cumin, sauté for additional minute or until fragrant, remove from heat, and set aside. In a food processor, blend the green onion mixture and the remaining ingredients until smooth. Taste and adjust seasonings as needed, you can also add more chipotle puree if you like spicy flavors. Serve with tortilla chips, crackers, or veggies.
Yield: 2 Cups

Sunshine Salsa

2 cups Roma tomatoes, deseeded and diced
1 cup yellow tomatoes, deseeded and diced
½ cup green pepper, fine diced
½ cup orange pepper, fine diced
½ cup red onion, fine diced
⅓ cup green onion, thinly sliced
¼ cup freshly chopped cilantro
2 Tbsp. freshly chopped parsley
1 green chili, minced
1 jalapeno, minced
1 Tbsp. garlic, minced
2 Tbsp. lime juice
1 tsp. salt
½ tsp. pepper

In a glass bowl, combine all of the ingredients, and toss well to combine. Cover and chill for 1 hour to allow the flavors to blend. Mix again before serving.

Yield: 4 Cups

Tomato Bruschetta

¾ cup olive oil, plus more for brushing
4 garlic cloves, minced
2 ½ cups fresh tomatoes, fine chopped
¼ cup fresh chopped basil
½ cup vegan parmesan cheese
Salt, to taste
1 French baguette, cut into½" thick slices

Heat the broiler and warm ¾ cup of olive oil in a large skillet over medium heat.
Add the garlic and stir until the garlic starts to brown—about 3 minutes, then let cool. Add the tomatoes and basil. Season with salt and keep warm. Brush both sides of each slice of bread with olive oil and place on a baking sheet. Sprinkle with salt, top each slice with the tomato mixture, top with vegan cheese and broil for 3 or 4 minutes.

Mushroom-Walnut Pâté

¼ cup water
¾ lb. sliced fresh mushrooms
½ medium onion, diced
2 cloves garlic, minced
¼ lb. firm tofu, mashed
½ cup walnuts
½ tsp. salt
¼ tsp. red pepper
1 green bell pepper, cored and seeded
½ loaf of French bread

Heat the water in a medium skillet over medium heat, then cook the mushrooms, onion, and garlic until soft, about 5 minutes. Put the vegetables and tofu in a food processor and purée until smooth. Add the walnuts, salt, and pepper and purée for another 5 minutes. Chill the pâté thoroughly. Slice the bell pepper into rings. Slices French bread and top with the pepper rings, then fill the rings with the pâté.

Makes 6 to 8 servings

...............Tuscan Stuffed Mushroom...

Spicy Sweet-Potato Fries

4medium sweet potato
3 Tbsp. olive oil
2 tsp. chili powder
2 tsp. salt
2 tsp. pepper
1 tsp. dry oregano
1 tsp. dry mustard
1 tsp. paprika

Preheat the oven to 425°F. Wash, scrub, dry, and cut sweet potatoes into ½-inch fries. Combine all the ingredients on a large baking sheet and toss well to coat all fries evenly. Bake for 25 to 30 minutes, tossing every 10 minutes. Many serve this with maple syrup for dipping.

Makes 5 cups

Tofu-Walnut 'Meatballs'

2 cups extra fine chopped walnuts
1 chopped onion
1 shredded carrot
1 chopped green pepper
4 cloves chopped garlic
Olive oil
12 oz. soft tofu
1 tsp. Sesame oil
1 tsp. Mustard
1 tsp. Oregano
1 tsp. Basil
2 cups bread crumbs
Salt and pepper to taste

Sauté walnuts, onion, carrot, pepper, and garlic in olive oil. In a large bowl, mix mashed soft tofu with sesame oil, mustard, oregano, and basil. Add sautéed items and mix well. Add enough bread crumbs to make a moldable mixture. Shape into balls and sauté.

Makes 4-6 servings

Tuscan Stuffed Mushroom

1 onion, diced
¼ red pepper, diced
1 celery stalk
2 tsp. basil
2 tsp. thyme
Salt and fresh pepper, to taste
2 tsp. paprika
Extra virgin olive oil for sautéing
2 slices vegan buttered toast, cut into crumbs
6 large mushrooms, washed and de-stemmed
Vegan Parmesan cheese for garnish

Set aside the toast, mushrooms, and cheese. Sauté all the other ingredients until the onions are transparent. Mix with the bread to create a stuffing and set aside. Place the mushrooms, gill side up, on an oiled baking sheet and fill with the stuffing. Bake at 350°F for 25 to 30 minutes, or until the mushrooms are tender. Top with the vegan Parmesan and enjoy!

Makes 4 to 6 servings

Stuffed Mushrooms

2 Tbsp. olive oil
8 large flat mushrooms
1 chopped onion
1 crushed garlic clove
¼ cup rolled oats
8oz. chopped tomatoes with herbs
salt and pepper sauce to taste
¼ cup diced pecans or pine nuts
½ cup soy parmesan

Preheat the oven to 375°F. Use a small amount of oil to grease a shallow baking dish large enough to hold a single layer of the mushroom caps and set aside. Remove the mushroom stalks and set the caps aside. Sauté the onion, garlic, and chopped mushroom stalks in the oil until lightly browned. Stir in oats and sauté for one minute. Add the tomatoes, salt and pepper sauce. Arrange the caps with the hole side up in the prepared baking dish. Divide the stuffing mixture between them and then top with the nuts and soy cheese. Bake for about 20 minutes, until browning on top.

Makes 8 Servings

Sautéed Mushrooms

2 Tbsp. extra virgin olive oil
2 cups button mushrooms
Salt, to taste
A few drops of lemon juice
Pinch of garlic paste
1 tsp. parsley, chopped

Heat the oil in a shallow pan. Sauté the mushrooms for about 4 to 5 minutes or until browned. Add all the ingredients together and sauté for another minute and serve hot.

'Crabless' Cakes

1 block firm tofu
¼ green pepper, finely chopped
¼ red pepper, finely chopped
½ red onion, finely chopped
2 medium carrots, grated
2 celery stalks, fine diced
½ cup dried cornbread crumbs
½ cup vegan mayonnaise
3 Tbsp. Dijon mustard
2 Tbsp. dill
1 Tbsp. dried basil
2 Tbsp. Cajun seasoning
1 tsp. white pepper
Salt, to taste
Japanese panko bread crumbs
for coating the cakes
Oil for frying

Crumble the tofu into a mixing bowl. Add all the ingredients, except for the panko and oil, and stir together well. If the mixture is too wet, add cornbread crumbs. If it's too dry, add a little more vegan mayonnaise. Using your hands, roll about ¼ cup of the mixture at a time into balls, then roll in the panko until coated. Flatten into cakes. Heat the oil in a large iron skillet until hot. Fry the cakes until golden brown.

Makes 3 servings

Faux Fish Cakes

1 lb. extra-firm tofu
2 cups cooked brown rice
1 small onion, minced
6 Tbsp. nutritional yeast flakes
2 Tbsp. minced celery
2 Tbsp. soy sauce
1 Tbsp. lemon juice
1 Tbsp. sea salt
½ tsp. dry mustard
½ tsp. dill weed
¼ tsp. white pepper
¼ tsp ground celery seed
¼ cup unbleached all-purpose flour

Mix the tofu, rice, onion, yeast and celery in a large bowl. Process the remaining ingredients, except for the flour, in a food processor until well blended. Add to mixtures together, along with the flour and hand mix well. Form into 4-oz. patties and broil or pan fry for about 4 minutes on each side.

Makes 8 servings

Oven Fries

6 potatoes cut into ¼-inch-thick slices
2 Tbsp. olive oil
Garlic powder, to taste
Ground sage, to taste
Paprika, to taste
Salt and pepper sprinkle
Preheat the oven to 475°F.

Place the potato slices on a cookie sheet and drizzle with the olive oil. Sprinkle with garlic powder, ground sage, and paprika; and mix with your hands until all the potatoes are coated. Bake for 10 minutes, then turn the fries over and bake another 10 minutes.

Makes 4 to 6 servings

New England Tofu Cakes

For the Cakes:
½ cup finely diced onions
2 tsp. minced garlic
2 lbs. firm tofu, crumbled
1 ½ Tbsp. cornstarch
¼ cup nutritional yeast
⅛ cup apple cider
¼ cup finely diced carrots
1 Tbsp. salt
½ tsp. ground white pepper
Juice of 1 lime

Sauté the onions and carrots until soft, about 3 to 5 minutes. Add the garlic and sauté 1 minute longer. Let cool completely. Add the remaining ingredients, mixing well. Let cool in the refrigerator for 30 minutes.

For the Old Bay Dredge
1 ½ cups finely ground breadcrumbs
3 Tbsp. seafood seasoning
1 Tbsp. salt
1 ½ cups all purpose flour
1 ½ cups soy milk
olive oil for frying

Mix the breadcrumbs, seasoning, and salt in a bowl and set aside. Using the tofu mixture, form small (approximately 2 oz.) cakes either by hand or with a scoop. Dredge in flour and coat with soy milk, then dredge in the seasoned bread-crumbs, coating well. Refrigerate for 30 minutes, until set. Put enough canola oil in a sauté pan to reach the middle of each cake and sauté over medium-high heat until browned on both sides and heated completely through. Serve with tartar or cocktail dipping sauce.

Makes 6 to 8 servings

Love Cakes

2 15-oz. cans cooked black beans
2 Tbsp. olive oil
2 Tbsp. diced yellow onion
2 garlic cloves, diced
1 tsp. ground cumin
1 tsp. kosher salt
1-4 cups masa de harina (a traditional Spanish "dough flour")
Tomatillo salsa for garnish
Slivered red onions for garnish

Rinse and drain the black beans in a colander. Heat 1 Tbsp. of the olive oil over medium heat in a sauté pan. Cook the onion, garlic, cumin, and salt until the onions are tender. Combine the beans and the sautéed onion mixture in a medium bowl and mash with a potato masher. Slowly add the masa de harina and continue mashing to form dough. Divide into 12 balls and form into little cakes. Place a large nonstick sauté pan over medium heat. Add the remaining olive oil and sauté the Love Cakes for approximately 5 to 7 minutes on each side, or until dark brown and crisp. Garnish with the salsa and the red onions.

Makes 6 servings

Mushrooms Rockefeller

4 Tbsp. olive oil
1 tsp. minced garlic
2 Tbsp. minced white onion
6 baby Portobello or large button mushrooms, cleaned, & stemmed
¼ cup frozen spinach, thawed
1 tsp. lemon juice
½ tsp. lemon zest
1 ½ Tbsp. pimiento
Salt and pepper, to taste

Lightly grease an 8x10-inch pan. Preheat the oven to 375°F. In a skillet over medium heat, heat the olive oil. Sauté the onion, garlic and mushrooms until soft. Remove mushrooms and add the spinach, lemon juice and zest, and pimiento and cook for another 2 minutes. Remove from the heat. Stuff the mushrooms with the spinach filling and bake for 15 minutes, or until the mushrooms are cooked.

Avocado & Mango Salsa

1 ripe mango, peeled and diced
1 ripe avocado, peeled and diced
1 Tbsp lime juice
2 Tbsp. walnut oil or other oil of choice
¼ tsp. kosher salt
½ cayenne pepper, seeded and minced
2 Tbsp. cilantro, finely chopped
3 Tbsp. red onion, minced

Gently toss all the ingredients together. It's that easy! Letting it set for a few minutes and then giving it another quick mix before serving will help the flavors blend.

Garlic-Potato Crostini

Creamy mashed potatoes top garlic bread in this simple and delicious appetizer.

4 medium yellow potatoes, peeled and cubed
1 Tbsp. vegan margarine, plus more for buttering the bread
2 Tbsp. vegan cream cheese
4 marinated artichoke hearts, minced
1-2 Tbsp. soy Parmesan cheese
½ cup grated vegan Monterey Jack cheese
1 onion, fine minced
3 Tbsp. fresh chives, minced
1 tsp. salt
⅛ tsp. pepper
1 French baguette, cut into ¼-inch slices
Garlic salt, to taste
Paprika, garnish

Boil the potatoes until tender, about 20 minutes. Drain and while still hot, add the vegan margarine, nondairy cream cheese, and artichoke hearts. Mash until smooth. Transfer to a container and refrigerate until cool. Add the cheeses, onion, chives, salt, and pepper to the potatoes and mix well. Set aside. Spread one side of each baguette slice with a thin layer of vegan margarine. Sprinkle with the garlic salt. Spread a heaping spoonful of the potato mixture on the opposite side of the slice and place it, potato-side-up, on a baking sheet. Repeat with all slices. Sprinkle a bit of the paprika on each slice. Bake at 400°F until crispy, about 10 minutes.

Makes 6 servings

Grilled Cajun Portobello With Avocado Crème

This can be used for an appetizer, entrée or for a Portobello Burger

For the Portobello Fillets:

2 Tbsp. hickory smoked salt smoked
2 Tbsp. paprika
2 Tbsp. garlic powder
1 Tbsp. onion powder
1 Tbsp. cayenne pepper
1 Tbsp. dried oregano leaves
1 Tbsp. thyme
4 portobello mushrooms, cleaned
4 Tbsp. olive oil

Combine the spices in a dish to making a Cajun rub. Lightly coat the mushrooms first with the olive oil and then with the rub.
Grill each side until cooked through.

For the Avocado Crème:
2 ripe avocados, peeled and pitted
¼ cup vegan mayonnaise
Juice of 1 lime
Salt and pepper, to taste

Combine ingredients in a blender until smooth. Add a little soy milk to make thinner if desired

Makes 4 servings

Pink Champagne

1 ½ cups ginger ale, chilled
1 ½ cups club soda, chilled
1 ½ cups white grape juice, chilled
¼ cup raspberry juice or cranberry juice, chilled

In a glass pitcher, stir together all of the ingredients. Serve immediately in your favorite stemware or over ice.

Yield: 4 Cups

Fruit Smoothie

Strawberry Banana Smoothie

1 cup apple juice
2 dates, pitted
1 cup strawberries, fresh or frozen
1 banana, peeled, and broken into 2-inch pieces

Blend the apple juice and dates for 1 minute. Add the remaining ingredients and blend an additional 1-2 minutes or until smooth and creamy. Serve.
*Variation: substitute other fruit or berries in the recipe, as desired.

Yield: 2 Cups

Banana Chocolate Shake

4 cups frozen bananas, cut into 2-inch chunks
1 cup soy milk
3 Tbsp. carob powder
2 Tbsp. maple syrup
1 Tbsp. vanilla

Remove the frozen banana chunks from the freezer and allow them to thaw for 5-10 minutes to soften slightly. Blend all ingredients for 2-3 minutes or until smooth. Serve immediately.
*Variation: add additional soy milk if you desire a thinner shake, or add almond or peppermint extract to vary the flavor, or add a little nut butter of choice for added flavor and creaminess.

Yield: 4 Cups

Orange Spice Apple Cider

2 Quarts apple cider
½ cup sugar
½ cup orange juice
2 cinnamon sticks
1 tsp. whole allspice
1 tsp. whole cloves
1 tsp. nutmeg

In a large pot, combine all of the ingredients, and simmer over medium heat for 10 minutes to blend the flavors. Strain the hot cider mixture and serve warm.

Yield: 8 ½ cup servings

Apple Carrot Drink

1 ½ lbs. carrots, washed well
1 lb. apples
1-inch piece ginger

Begin by trimming the ends off the carrots and then cut them into 4-inch pieces that will fit through your juicer. Next, core the apples, discarding the seeds, and cut the apples into pieces that will fit through your juicer. Remove some of the peel from the piece of ginger. Turn on your juicer, and juice in the following order: half of the carrots, the piece of ginger, all of the apple, and then the remaining half of the carrots. This will allow the flavors to blend while juicing.

Yield: 2 Cups

Strawberry Lemonade

1 pint strawberries
1 ¾ cups unbleached sugar
1 ½ cups water
3 ½ cups lemon juice
ice

In a blender, puree the strawberries until smooth. Pass the pureed strawberries through a sieve to remove the seeds and set aside. In a large pitcher, place the sugar and water, and stir well to dissolve the sugar. Add the lemon juice and strawberry puree to the mixture and stir well to combine. Chill. Serve in ice-filled glasses.

Yield: 2 Quarts

Warm Spiced Cranberry Apple Drink

2 Quarts cranberry juice
2 ½ cups apple juice
⅓ cup sugar
2 - 3-inch cinnamon sticks
1 tsp. allspice
1 orange, sliced
8-10 whole cloves

In a large pot, combine the cranberry juice, apple juice, sugar, cinnamon sticks, and allspice, and bring to a boil. Reduce heat and simmer for 10 minutes. Stud the slices of orange with the whole cloves and set aside. Strain the juice to remove the spices. Transfer it to a punch bowl, garnish it with the orange slices, and serve warm.

Yield: 10 ½ cup servings

SALADS & DRESSINGS

....................Cucumber Salad.......

Cucumber Salad

This is a fun and elegant recipe that is sure to catch your guest's attention. Once you learn this gourmet culinary process, you will be able to do many different exciting combinations. It's so easy and the possibilities are endless. This recipe will make 4 salads.

For the Cucumber Cylinders:

2 cucumbers

Take the cucumbers and slice a couple good slices out of the middle. I use a slicer, but you can use a knife or using a wide vegetable peeler will give you a consistent slice. We will save the rest of the cucumber for the filling. We are going to curve the cucumber together and then you can attach them together with a decorative pick. What I do is just do an angle cut on each end and then hook them together.

For the filling
1 C Cucumber (peeled and diced)
1 Avocado (small ½ slivers)
¼ cup onion (small ½ slivers)
4 Strawberries (thin sliced)
1 Green Apple diced
¼ C dried cranberries
1 Tbsp Lemon juice

Take the diced apples and splash with the lemon juice and mix in well. This will keep them from turning brown. For the diced cucumbers, I use the leftovers from the slices that I took out of the cucumbers. For the strawberries, slice off the stems and then do a thin flat slice so you can get the strawberry shape. If you have a dehydrator, I also like to dry the strawberries to the dryness of a dried fruit. Gently mix in all the additional ingredients and gently place in the cucumber cylinder. You can also add nuts for a crunchy addition.

Splash with this infused olive oil.

Basil Infused Olive Oil
¼ cup olive oil
1 tsp Crushed Garlic
¼ tsp Sea Salt
2 Tbsp Fresh Basil
1 Tbsp Cilantro
⅛ tsp red pepper flakes

For the infused olive oil, I use a good extra virgin cold pressed olive oil. I would rather use a bold flavor for this than light oil. We want the flavor popping. Add all the ingredients together and blend in a blender for a good minute. Splash this on the plate and salad.

Garnish with fresh dill or Cilantro

*Optional: add some imitation bacon slivers, chicken strips or nuts for a flavor enhancer

Vegan Caesar Dressing

¼ cup whole garlic cloves
4 Tbsp. salt or to taste
2 Tbsp. Dijon mustard
1 lbs. firm tofu, cut into cubes
2 cups organic canola oil
2 cups extra-virgin olive oil
4 cups lemon juice

Combine all the ingredients in a large bucket and buzz with an immersion blender until smooth.

Makes ¹/₂ gallon

Ranch Dressing

1 cup Nayonaise
1 cup Veganaise
½ cup soy milk
1 ½ tsp. garlic powder
1 tsp. onion powder
1 tsp. pepper and ½ tsp. salt or to taste
1 rounded Tbsp. fresh chopped parsley
1 Tbsp apple cider or vinegar (optional)
½ tsp. dill

Put all ingredients in the blender and blend until creamy.

Makes approximately one cup

Thousand Island Dressing

1 cup vegan mayonnaise
⅓ cup ketchup
½ tsp. onion powder
¼ tsp. salt
⅛ tsp. garlic powder
3 Tbsp. sweet pickle relish
2 Tbsp. minced stuffed green olives

Blend the ingredients thoroughly in a mixing bowl or blender.

Makes 2 cups

Soy Vegan Mayonnaise

12 oz tofu, firm
1 Tbsp. lemon juice
1 Tbsp. Dijon mustard
1 Tbsp. sugar
½ tsp. salt
⅓ cup olive oil

In a food processor, place all of the ingredients, except the olive oil, and process for 2 minutes to form a smooth puree. While the machine is running, drizzle in the olive oil, and continue to process an additional 2-3 minutes or until light and creamy. Taste and adjust seasonings, as needed to suit personal taste. Transfer to an airtight container and store in the refrigerator.

Yield: 2 Cups

Almond Mayonnaise

⅓ cup raw almonds
1 Tbsp. nutritional yeast flakes
1 tsp. lecithin granules
¼ tsp. onion powder
¼ tsp. garlic powder
¼ tsp. salt
½ cup safflower oil
3 Tbsp. water
4 tsp. apple cider
4 tsp. lemon juice

Begin by blanching the almonds. In a small saucepan, place 2 inches of water, and bring to a boil. Add the almonds and cook for 1 minute to blanch them. Remove the saucepan from the heat and set aside for 3 minutes to cool. Remove the almonds from the water, squeeze each almond between your thumb and forefinger to remove their skins, and set them aside for 5 minutes to dry and cool. Place the almonds in a blender and process for 1-2 minutes to finely grind them. Add the nutritional yeast, lecithin, onion powder, garlic powder, kelp, and salt, and process for 30 seconds to combine. In a small measuring cup, combine the oil and water, and add the mixture to the blender in a slow stream while the machine is running. Scrape down the sides of the container, add the vinegar and lemon juice, and continue to process the mixture an additional 1-2 minutes or until thickened. Chill for 30 minutes or more before using.

Yield: 1 ¼ cups

Vegan Mayonnaise #2

3 Tbsp. lemon juice
½ cup soya milk
¼ tsp. salt
¼ tsp. paprika
¼ tsp. prepared mustard
6 Tbsp. vegetable oil

Put all the ingredients except the oil in a blender. Blend on the lowest speed. Add the oil one drop at a time until the mixture starts to thicken. Do not rush this or it will not emulsify! Continue blending until thickened and smooth. Transfer to a jar and store in the refrigerator.

Asparagus and Noodle Salad

8 oz. linguine noodles
¾ lb. asparagus, cut diagonally into 1 inch pieces
½ cup orange juice
2 Tbsp. soy sauce
1 Tbsp. sesame oil
2 tsp. vinegar (optional)
1 tsp. minced roasted garlic
1 tsp. ginger powder
1 tsp. grated orange peel
¼ tsp. brown sugar
Dash pepper sauce, or to taste
½ cup green onions fine sliced
Cook the noodles according to the package

directions. Blanch off asparagus right in with the cooking noodles. Pour the noodles into the colander and drain. Meanwhile combine the remaining ingredients in a large bowl and mix well. Add the noodles and asparagus and stir gently until well blended. Refrigerate for several hours or overnight, stirring occasionally. Stir again before serving and serve cold.

Makes 4 servings

Red Potato Salad

2 ½ lbs. red potatoes
½ cup olive oil
2 Tbsp. Dijon mustard
2 Tbsp. white wine vinegar (optional)
4 Tbsp. vegan mayo
1 tsp. garlic powder
Salt and pepper, to taste
½ cup chopped red pepper
½ cup chopped celery
⅓ cup chopped red onion

Wash and quarter the potatoes. Cook in salted water until just tender. Drain and let air dry until completely cool. This tightens them up. Whisk together the olive oil, mustard, vinegar, vegan mayonnaise, garlic powder, salt, and pepper. In a large bowl, gently fold the chopped vegetables into the potatoes. Add the dressing, tossing to coat. Season to taste.

Makes 6 servings

Tangy Black Bean and Corn Salad

2-15 oz. cans black beans, rinsed and drained
1 ½ cups frozen corn kernels
1 avocado, peeled, pitted, and diced
1 red bell pepper, diced
2 tomatoes, seeded and diced
6 green onions, minced
¼ cup fresh cilantro, chopped
⅓ cup freshly squeezed lime juice
½ cup olive oil
1 clove garlic, minced
1 tsp. salt
⅛ tsp. red pepper

In a salad bowl, combine the beans, corn, avocado, bell pepper, tomatoes, green onions, and cilantro. Place the lime juice, olive oil, garlic, salt, and cayenne pepper into a small jar. Cover with a lid and shake to mix thoroughly. Pour the vinaigrette over the salad ingredients and stir gently to coat. Serve immediately or refrigerate for later, stirring again before serving.

Makes 4 servings

Thai Peanut Dressing

½ cup peanut butter
⅓ cup peanut oil
¼ cup lime juice
3 Tbsp. water
2 Tbsp. toasted sesame oil
1 Tbsp. maple syrup
1 tsp. garlic, minced
¼ tsp. cayenne pepper

In a blender or food processor, place all of the ingredients, and blend until smooth.

Yield: 1 ½ cups

Asian Fusion Salad

This colorful salad is perfect for a main course or as a starter for an Asian meal.

1 head red leaf lettuce
1 cup snow peas
1 large cucumber
1 sweet red bell pepper
1 ½ cups bean sprouts
2 carrots
8 oz. flavored baked tofu of your choice of teriyaki, sesame or ginger
1 Tbsp. balsamic vinegar (optional)
1 tsp. soy sauce
1 tsp. sesame oil
¼ tsp. chili sauce

Wash and tear the lettuce into bite-sized pieces. Drain thoroughly and place in a large salad bowl. Trim the tips from the snow peas and cut on a diagonal slant into 1-inch slices. Peel the cucumber and julienne. Cut the red pepper in half and remove the seeds and pith. Cut it into thin slices and then cut the slices diagonally into thirds. Rinse and drain the bean sprouts. Julienne the carrots and blanch them by submerging them in boiling water for 3 to 4 minutes. Rinse with cold water and drain. Add the snow peas, cucumber, red pepper, bean sprouts, and carrots to the salad and make an indentation in the center of the salad. Cut the tofu into ¼-inch slices and then cut crosswise to make bite-sized pieces. Stir together the vinegar, soy sauce, sesame oil, and chili sauce. Pour over the tofu and toss. Add the tofu mixture to the center of the salad just before serving.

Makes 4 entrees or 8 side servings

Blueberry & Wild Rice Salad

A light citrus dressing goes perfectly with the fruit and wild rice in this satisfying summer salad.

1 cup wild rice, washed
2 cups vegetable broth
⅓ cup toasted, chopped pecans
½ cup dried cranberries
¾ cup chopped dried apricots
½ cup chopped red onion
¼ cup lime juice
2 Tbsp. apricot nectar
1 ½ tsp. grated fresh ginger
1 tsp. grated lime peel
6 Tbsp. olive oil
Salt and pepper, to taste
1 cup blueberries

Combine the rice with the vegetable broth and enough water to cover by 1 inch in a medium saucepan. Bring to a boil. Reduce the heat and simmer, covered, until the rice is tender, about 40 minutes. Let completely cool. Stir in the pecans, cranberries, apricots, and red onion. Set aside. In a small bowl, whisk together the lime juice, apricot nectar, ginger, and lime peel. Gradually whisk in the olive oil. Season with salt and pepper. Pour over the rice and mix well. Gently fold in the blueberries. Let sit for 10 minutes before serving.

Makes 4 to 6 servings

Eggless Veggie Salad

1 lb. firm tofu, dry
½ cup soy mayonnaise
1 ½ tsp. lemon juice
½ tsp. salt
¼ tsp. onion powder
¼ tsp. turmeric
⅛ tsp. pepper
¼ cup red pepper, fine diced
½ cup celery, diced
⅓ cup radishes, thin slice & dice
¼ cup green onions, fine sliced
¼ cup freshly chopped parsley

Wrap the block of tofu in a clean, lint-free towel. Place a colander in the sink or over a bowl, place the towel-wrapped tofu in the colander, and place a large plate over the top of it. Place a large can or something very heavy on top of the plate and leave tofu to sit for 20 minutes. This technique makes the texture of the tofu much firmer. **It is called pressing the tofu.** Using your fingers, crumble the pressed tofu into a bowl. Add soy mayonnaise, lemon juice, salt, onion powder, turmeric, and pepper, and stir well to thoroughly coat the tofu. Add the remaining ingredients and stir well. Cover and chill for 1 hour to allow the flavors to blend. The color of the eggless egg salad will turn more yellow also as it chills. Use as a filling for sandwiches, salads, and vegetables.

Yield: 3 Cups

Zesty Cabbage Slaw

1 ½ cups shredded green cabbage
1 medium-sized carrot, grated
½ small onion, finely chopped
2 Tbsp. fine diced peppers
2 Tbsp. lemon juice
¾ cup vegan mayonnaise
1 Tbsp. ground celery
2 Tbsp. sugar

Salt and pepper, to taste.
In a large bowl, combine all the wet ingredients with the spices and whip. Add the cabbage carrot, onion and peppers and mix well.

Tomato and Orzo Pasta Salad

12 oz. orzo or other dry pasta of choice
1 cup yellow pear tomatoes, cut in half
1 cup cherry tomatoes, cut in half
1 cup orange or yellow pepper, diced
1 cup celery, diced
1 cup English cucumber, and diced
½ cup black olives, sliced
⅓ cup lemon juice
¼ cup olive oil
¼ cup vegetable stock or water
2 Tbsp. Dijon mustard
¼ tsp. sea salt
¼ tsp. red pepper
¼ tsp. crushed red pepper flakes
⅓ cup freshly chopped basil
¼ cup freshly chopped parsley
3 Tbsp. freshly chopped dill

In a large pot of salted, boiling water, cook the orzo for 5-7 minutes or until al dente. Drain, rinse with cold water, drain well again, and set the orzo aside to cool. In a large bowl, place the pear and cherry tomatoes, orange pepper, celery, cucumber, and black olives, and toss gently. In a small bowl, place the lemon juice, olive oil, vegetable stock, mustard, salt, pepper, and crushed red pepper flakes, and whisk well to combine. Add the herbs and whisk well to thoroughly incorporate them into the mixture. Add the cooled orzo and dressing to the vegetable mixture and toss gently to combine. Cover and chill for 30 minutes or more to allow the flavors to blend. Gently toss the salad again before serving.

Yield: 3 Quarts

SOUPS & SAUCES

Lentil Vegetable Soup

Walnut-Portobello Gravy

5 medium Portobello mushrooms, chopped
1 cup walnuts
¼ cup diced onions
2 Tbsp. olive oil
1 cup vegetable stock
2 cloves garlic, minced
Salt and fresh pepper, to taste
Extra Water, if needed
¼ cup tamari, or to taste
¼ cup olive oil, or as needed
¼ cup nutritional yeast

Sauté the mushrooms, walnuts, and onions in the olive oil for 4 to 5 minutes. Add the vegetable stock and simmer until the walnuts are tender, about 10 minutes. Remove from the heat and let cool for 5 minutes. Place all the ingredients in a blender and blend until smooth.

Makes 4 to 6 servings

Sweet 'n' Sour Glaze

1 cup tomato juice
1 cup pineapple juice
½ cup orange juice
2 Tbsp. soy sauce
½ cup lemon juice
2 Tbsp. hot sauce
¼ oz. ginger
¼ cup sugar
1 cup sake
2 Tbsp. ketchup
2 Tbsp. plum sauce
Cornstarch & water slurry

Place all the ingredients in a pot and bring to a boil. Simmer for 10 minutes, then thicken with slurry and strain through a fine mesh. Serve hot or cold.

Singapore Sauce

Serve this spicy sauce with Singapore Street Noodles.
¼ cup curry powder
Pinch of turmeric (optional)
¼ cup light soy sauce
1 cup vegetarian oyster sauce
¼ cup chili sauce
¼ cup ketchup

Mix well until the powders are well dissolved.

Makes 4 servings

Vietnamese Spicy Red Sauce

1 tsp. sugar syrup
⅓ tsp. salt
1 Tbsp. coconut juice
1 red chili, finely minced
1 tsp. sugar
1 tsp. julienne radish

Thoroughly combine all the ingredients except radishes. Garnish top of sauce with the radish.

Tasty Tartar Sauce

½ lb. soft or medium-firm tofu
¼ cup safflower oil
Juice of ½ lemon or 2 Tbsp pickle juice
½ tsp. salt
1 tsp. prepared mustard
¼ cup sweet pickle relish

Blend together the tofu, oil, lemon juice, salt, and mustard in a food processor until smooth. Stir in the pickle relish and it's ready to serve.

Makes about 1 ½ cups

Milligan's Spicy Soup

1 ½ cups chopped onion
3 celery stalk, chopped
1 small chili, seeded and chopped (or a pinch of cayenne, to taste)
1 tsp. turmeric
1 Tbsp. ground coriander seeds
4 cups vegetable stock
2 cup soy milk
1 Tbsp. salt
2 medium carrot, chopped
2 large potato, cut into small cubes
1 medium red and green bell pepper, chopped
1 firm diced tomato
½ tsp. coconut extract (optional)

4 Tbsp. fresh lemon or lime juice
3 tsp. chopped fresh cilantro

In a medium soup pot, sauté the onions and celery in a little bit of the broth. When the onions are translucent, add the chili, turmeric and ground coriander. Sauté for one more minute. Add the stock, soy milk, salt, carrot and potato. Bring to a boil, reduce heat, cover and simmer for 10 minutes. Add the pepper, tomato and coconut extract. Simmer gently for another 10 minutes or until the vegetables are tender. Then add the lemon or lime juice and cilantro.

Makes 6 servings

Southwestern Dumpling Soup

For the Soup:

15-oz. can kidney beans
15-oz. can black beans
3 cups vegetable broth
24 oz. chopped tomatoes
3 tsp. chili powder
3 garlic cloves, minced
10 oz. frozen corn
2 large carrots, sliced
1 cup chopped onion
4 oz. chopped green chili peppers
Hot sauce and salt, to taste

Combine all the ingredients in a slow cooker. Cover and cook on low for 8 to 10 hours.

For the Dumplings:

⅓ cup flour
¼ cup cornmeal
1 tsp. baking powder
Pinch of salt & cayenne pepper
Pinch of dry mustard
2 ½ Tbsp. soy milk
1 Tbsp. olive oil

In a small bowl, combine the flour, cornmeal, baking powder, salt, and pepper. In another bowl, combine the soy milk and oil. Add to the flour mixture and stir until just combined. Turn the slow cooker to high and drop the dumpling batter by the teaspoonful over the soup. Cover and cook for 30 to 40 minutes, or until the dumplings are cooked.

Makes 4 to 6 servings

Roaring Ratatouille Soup

1 Tbsp. olive oil
1 large onion, diced
1 bay leaf
½ cup tomato juice
3 cloves garlic, crushed
1 Tbsp. dried basil
1 Tbsp. dried marjoram
1 Tbsp. dried oregano
Dash of ground rosemary
1 tsp. salt
½ tsp. red pepper
1 medium zucchini, sliced
1 green bell pepper, chopped
1 red bell pepper, chopped
1 small eggplant, cut into small cubes
2 large tomatoes, cut into medium wedges
5 Tbsp. tomato paste

Heat the olive oil and a little water in a large saucepan over medium heat. Sauté the onion until translucent. Add the bay leaf, and tomato juice and stir well. Then add the garlic, herbs, salt, and pepper and mix until well blended. Cover the saucepan and simmer for 10 minutes over low heat. Add the zucchini and peppers stir well, cover, and simmer for another 5 minutes. Add the eggplant, tomatoes, and tomato paste and stir again. Cover and continue to simmer until the vegetables are tender, about 8 minutes more. Serve over rice or with crusty French bread. Optional add pastas.

Makes 4 to 5 servings

Pasta e Fagioli

2 stalks celery, diced
1 large onion, diced
2 stalks parsley, chopped
2 cloves garlic, minced
1 Tbsp. salt
Pinch red pepper
¼ cup olive oil
2 - 14.5-oz. cans cannelloni beans,
including liquid
1 - 15-oz. can diced tomatoes, including juice
4 cups water
½ lb. macaroni, uncooked
1 head of endive, coarsely chopped

In a large pot over medium heat, sauté the celery, onion, parsley, garlic, salt, and red pepper in the olive oil until the celery and onion are soft. Add the beans, tomatoes, and water, bring to a boil, then reduce the heat to medium-low and simmer, uncovered, for 45 minutes. Add the macaroni and endive return to a boil, and cook for 10 minutes. Serve hot.

Makes 4 servings

Pasta e Fagioli #2

½ cup water or vegetable stock
2 onions, chopped
1 large bell pepper, diced
2 carrots, sliced
2 celery stalks, sliced
½ lb. (about 2 cups) mushrooms, sliced
1 - 15oz. can chopped tomatoes
1 - 15oz. can pinto beans, drained
1 tsp. paprika
½ tsp. red pepper
2 Tbsp. low-sodium soy sauce
8 ounces rigatoni (or similar pasta)

In a large pot, heat the water or stock. Braise the onions for 3 minutes, then add the pepper, carrots, and celery and cook for 5 minutes over medium heat. Add the mushrooms, cover the pan, and cook an additional 5 minutes, stirring occasionally. Add the tomatoes, pinto beans, paprika, pepper, and soy sauce, then cover and cook 10 to 15 minutes. Cook the pasta in a large pot of boiling water until just tender. Rinse and drain, then add it to the vegetable mixture.

Makes 10 servings

ClamFree Chowder

2 Tbsp. oliveoil
1 medium onion
¼ cup diced carrots
3 celery stalks
2 cups water
2 cups soymilk
½ lb. medium tofu, crumbled
2 tsp. sea salt & pepper to taste
½ tsp. garlic
½ tsp. celery seed
2 large potatoes, peeled and cubed
(about 2 cups)

Chop the onion, carrots, and celery. Heat the oil in a large cooking pot. Add the onion, carrots and celery and sauté for 15 minutes add garlic. Add the water and soymilk and stir. Add the tofu, salt, pepper, and celery seed and bring to a boil. Add the potatoes and let the chowder simmer until the potatoes are soft.
Tip: Use sea salt instead of regular salt to really bring out the "chowder" flavor.

Makes 8 servings

Gumbo Relish Soup

6 Tbsp. olive oil
6 Tbsp. whole wheat flour
3 cloves garlic, minced
1 ½ Tbsp. chopped fresh parsley leaves
¾ tsp. cayenne pepper
1 ½ tsp. oregano
1 ½ tsp. paprika
1 ½ tsp. file spice
2 tsp. sea salt, to taste
3 cups chopped green bell pepper
3 cups chopped red pepper
1 ½ cups green onion (green and white parts)
1 ½ cups chopped yellow onion
8 cups brown stock
3 bay leaves
3 sprigs fresh thyme

Prepare a roux by heating the oil and adding the flour. Once the roux is light brown, add the garlic and sauté for 2 to 3 minutes until translucent. Add the chopped parsley, cayenne pepper, oregano, paprika, file, and salt. Sauté. Add the chopped red and green bell peppers and green and yellow onion and sauté for 5 to 10 minutes. Add the stock, bay leaf, and fresh thyme to the pot and simmer for 20 to 25 minutes. Remove the bay leaf and thyme.

Makes 8 servings

Blue Ribbon Chili

3 Tbsp. vegetable oil
2 pounds TVP drained
2 large sweet onions, diced
1 green bell pepper, diced
Fresh garlic to taste, minced
2 4-ounce cans mushrooms
¼ cup chili powder (or to taste)
Salt and pepper to taste
¼ tsp. cayenne pepper
2 Tbsp. ground cumin
1 - 14ounce can tomato sauce
2 - 28ounce cans whole peeled tomatoes, with liquid
1 - 52ounce can red kidney beans, drained and rinsed
3 Tbsp. sugar

Sauté the TVP for 3 minutes; add the onions, green pepper, garlic, mushrooms, chili powder, salt, pepper, cayenne pepper, and cumin. Cook until the vegetables are tender, about 5 to 7 minutes. Add the tomato sauce, whole tomatoes, beans, and sugar. Simmer for about 1 hour.

Makes 8 servings

Slow Cooker Chili

2 Tbsp. olive oil
6 garlic cloves, minced
1 cup chopped white onion
1 lb. veggie burger crumbles
Salt & pepper flakes, to taste
3 Tbsp. chili powder
2 Tbsp. cumin
1 tsp. oregano
1 bay leaf
28-oz. can diced tomatoes
1 ½ cups vegetable stock
6 oz. tomato paste
28 oz. black beans, drained and rinsed
16 oz. pinto beans, drained and rinsed
16 oz. kidney beans, drained and rinsed

Heat the oil in a large skillet over medium heat. Cook the garlic, onion, veggie burger crumbles, and red pepper flakes until the onions are soft. Add the chili powder and cumin and cook for an additional 2 minutes, or until fragrant. Place in a slow cooker with the remaining ingredients, stirring to combine. Cover and cook on low for 6 to 8 hours.

Makes 6 to 8 servings

Magnificent Minestrone

3 Tbsp. soy sauce
1 tsp. garlic powder
1 lb. tofu, cut into ½-inch cubes
1 medium-sized onion, diced
2 carrots, sliced
1 medium-sized zucchini, sliced
2 Tbsp. olive oil
1 - 28oz. can tomatoes, diced
4 cups water
2 cups tomato juice
2 tsp. basil
1 tsp. oregano
½ tsp. salt
¼ tsp. pepper
3 oz. macaroni
1 - 15oz. can kidney beans

Preheat the oven to 375°F. Mix together the soy sauce and ½ tsp. of the garlic powder and mix into the tofu cubes. Bake the tofu on an oiled cookie sheet for 10 minutes. Turn the cubes and bake 5 minutes more. Set aside. Sauté the onion, carrots, and zucchini in the olive oil for about 10 minutes. Combine the sautéed vegetables in a soup pot with the tomatoes, water, tomato juice, basil, oregano, remaining garlic powder, salt, and pepper. Bring to a boil and add the pasta. Simmer for 15 minutes, then add the kidney beans and browned tofu cubes. Serve when the beans and tofu are heated through. If you want to thicken it a bit, Add tomato paste

Makes 11 1-cup servings

Classic Corn Chowder

3 cups corn kernels, divided
8 cups water
¼ cup vegan margarine
2 Tbsp. minced shallots
2 tsp. minced garlic
1 yellow onion, diced
1 red & 1 green pepper, diced
2 julienne leeks
2 stalks celery, diced
1 cup vegan chicken bouillon
2 carrots, diced
1 potato, diced
1 Tbsp. vegan cream cheese
4 Tbsp. yellow corn meal
1 tsp. chopped fresh sage
1 tsp. chopped thyme
Salt and pepper, to taste

Place 1 cup each of the corn and water in a pot, bring to a boil, then reduce heat and simmer for 15 minutes. Puree and press through a sieve, saving the corn "cream." Melt the margarine in a large pot. Add the shallots, garlic, onion, peppers, leeks, and celery and cook until soft. Add 6 cups of the water, the bouillon, carrots, and potato. Bring to a boil, the lower the heat and simmer for 20 minutes. Beat the vegan cream cheese, 1 cup of the water, the corn meal, and the corn "cream" until smooth. Add to the soup along with the remaining corn, herbs, salt and pepper.

Makes 6-8 servings

Sri Lankan Style Curried Mixed-Bean Soup

3 cups dried, mixed beans
8 cups water
1 medium onion, peeled diced
5 garlic cloves
2 carrots
½ tsp. fennel seed
⅔ cup shredded, unsweetened coconut
1 - 6oz. can tomato paste
1 tsp. cumin
2 tsp. ground coriander seed
½ tsp. fenugreek
½ tsp. ground mustard seed
½ tsp. cinnamon
1 tsp. ginger
½ tsp. cardamom
½ tsp. cloves
½ tsp. cayenne pepper

Chopped parsley (optional), for garnish
Thoroughly wash and clean the mixed beans and place them in a slow cooker, set on medium heat, with 6 cups of boiling water. Cook overnight or for about 8 hours. Place the onion, garlic, carrots, fennel seed, coconut and 2 cups cold water in a blender and blend at high speed until smooth. Add the onion mixture to the slow cooker and set the heat to 'high'. Add the remaining ingredients and mix thoroughly. Cook for another 4 or more hours, stirring occasionally. Add extra water, if needed, to reach the desired consistency. Garnish the soup with chopped parsley.

Lentil-Vegetable Soup

2 stalks celery
2 carrots
1 large onion
3 cloves garlic
1 Tbsp. olive oil
2 bay leaves
7 cups water
1 Tbsp. Italian herb mix
1 ½-2 cups green lentils
3 red potatoes (optional)
1 bunch spinach
1 tsp. salt
3 Tbsp. apple cider

Chop the celery, carrots, onion, and garlic. Heat the oil in a large soup pot and add the vegetables and bay leaves. Cook on medium heat until the vegetables are soft. Add the water, herbs, and lentils. Cook over medium to high heat for 45 minutes, adding more water as needed (2 or more cups will evaporate during cooking). Chop the potatoes into small cubes, if using. Add them to the soup and cook until soft, about 10 to 12 minutes. Add the spinach leaves and cook for about 2 more minutes, just long enough to wilt the leaves. Remove from the heat. Stir in the apple cider and leave covered until ready to serve.

Makes approximately 8 servings

Butternut Squash Soup

1 cup carrots, chopped
1 cup celery, chopped
6 sprigs fresh parsley
4 sprigs fresh thyme
1 Tbsp. whole peppercorns
1 bay leaf
1 cup white wine or apple cider
5 cups water
2 large onions, diced, with ¼ cup reserved
3 cups butternut squash, peeled and diced
Salt and freshly ground red pepper, to taste
Pinch of nutmeg, to taste
2 Tbsp. white truffle oil, (optional)
¼ cup Corn Nuts snack, plain flavor, coarsely crushed, for garnish

Place the carrot, celery, parsley, thyme, peppercorns, bay leaf, white wine, water, and all but ¼ cup of the onions in a large pot, bring to a boil, and then reduce the heat and simmer for 2 to 3 hours. Strain the soup, discard the pulp, and return the liquid to the pot. Add the squash and remaining onion to the pot and cook over medium heat until the squash is tender. Transfer the squash, onion, and one cup of the liquid (reserve the remaining liquid in a separate container) to a blender or food processor and blend until smooth. Season it with salt, pepper, and nutmeg. Add the truffle oil, if desired. Blend again until oil is incorporated. Pour the purée back into the pot and add some of the reserved liquid, stirring to achieve desired consistency. Ladle the soup into bowls and sprinkle Corn Nuts over each.

Makes 4 servings

Chef Anthony's Louisiana Gumbo

4 cups water
1 cup roux*
3 cups chopped onion
1 red & 1 green pepper, chopped
3 stalks celery, chopped
2 cloves fresh garlic
64 oz vegetable broth
Salt & red pepper, to taste
¼ cup Cajun seasoning, to taste
1 pkg. frozen chopped okra
1 lb. vegan chicken, chopped (optional)
½ cup chopped fresh flat-leaf parsley
½ cup chopped green onion tops
Cooked rice

Bring the water to a boil in a large pot. Add the roux and boil for 30 minutes. Add the onion, bell pepper, and celery. Cook until softened. Add the garlic, broth, salt, red pepper, and Cajun seasoning. Bring to a boil and cook for 5 minutes. Lower the heat and simmer for 1 hour. Add the okra and cook for an additional hour. Add the vegan chicken and cook for 30 minutes. Stir in the parsley and green onion tops 15 minutes before serving. Serve over the cooked rice. Or mix in the rice and simmer a few minutes.

Makes 4 to 6 servings

*Note: For the roux, combine equal parts of flour and oil in a heavy pot over medium-high heat. Cook, stirring constantly, for 30 minutes, or until chocolate brown, being careful not to burn. (If it does burn, you'll have to throw it out and start over.)

Beefless Stew

good

1 cup dry "beef" style textured vegetable protein chunks
1 cup boiling water
1 tsp. lemon juice
1 medium-sized onion, chopped
1 clove garlic, minced
1 Tbsp. olive oil
2 Tbsp Vegan Beef Base
4 cups water
1 - 14oz. can diced tomatoes
1 Tbsp. Worcestershire sauce
2 small bay leaves
2 tsp. salt
½ tsp. pepper
1 vegetable bouillon cube
1 tsp. sugar
6 carrots, chopped
3 potatoes, cut into bite-sized pieces
1 - 10oz. pkg. frozen peas
2 Tbsp. cornstarch, dissolved in a small amount of water slurry

Reconstitute the beef-style chunks in the boiling water and lemon juice. Let stand for 5 to 10 minutes. Brown the onion and garlic in the oil, add the chunks, and continue browning. Add the water, tomatoes, Worcestershire sauce, beef base, bay leaves, salt, pepper, bouillon cube, and sugar and simmer for 1 hour. Add the carrots and potatoes. Cook another 30 minutes. Thicken with the slurry. Add the peas right before serving

Makes 6 servings

Tortilla Soup

1 Tbsp. vegetable oil

1 medium onion, diced

2 cloves garlic, minced

2 chipotle or fresh jalapeño peppers, seeded and chopped

1 pasilla or Anaheim pepper, seeded and chopped

1 - 28oz. can crushed tomatoes

4 cups vegan chicken broth

Vegetable oil for frying

12 white corn tortillas, cut into thin strips

2 tsp. salt, plus extra to sprinkle on the tortillas

Juice from one freshly squeezed lime

2 ripe avocados, cut into small chunks

4 Tbsp. nondairy sour cream

1 green onion, chopped

2 sprigs cilantro, chopped

Heat the oil in a skillet over medium heat. Add the onion and garlic and sauté until golden. In a blender, purée the onion, garlic, peppers, and half the can of tomatoes. Transfer the purée, along with the remaining half can of crushed tomatoes and the broth, to a large pot. Bring to a boil. Lower the heat and simmer, uncovered, stirring occasionally, for 20 minutes. Meanwhile, heat the oil for frying in a heavy pot over medium-high heat or in a deep-fryer. Add the tortilla strips and fry until golden brown. Transfer the strips to a paper-towel-lined plate and sprinkle with salt. Just before serving, add 2 tsp. salt and the lime juice to the soup and stir. Divide the avocado chunks into four soup bowls, ladle the soup over them, and garnish each with 1 Tbsp. nondairy sour cream, fried tortilla strips, green onions, and cilantro. Serve immediately.

Makes 4 servings

Cajun Vegetable Gumbo

2 lbs. collard greens washed and stemmed

¼ cup vegetable oil

¼ cup flour

2 large onions, finely diced

1 green bell pepper, finely diced

4 stalks celery, finely diced

1 - 16oz. can tomatoes chopped

2 Tbsp hot sauce

3 bay leaves

1 tsp. file powder (optional)

Cayenne pepper, to taste

½ tsp. each thyme, oregano, and basil

¼ cup fresh parsley, chopped

3 garlic cloves, minced

Salt and pepper, to taste

6 cups vegetable broth

1 - 10oz. package frozen okra

1 - 16oz. can kidney beans, drained and rinsed

2 cups cooked white rice

Place the greens in a large soup pot with enough water to just cover the greens. Bring to a boil and cook for 15 minutes. Drain, reserving 2 cups of the cooking water. On a cutting board, coarsely chop the greens and set aside. In a small saucepan over medium-low heat, whisk ¼ cup oil and the flour together and cook, stirring constantly, until the roux is a dark reddish-brown. Remove the pan from the heat and set aside. In the large soup pot, sauté the onions, bell pepper, celery, and tomatoes for about 5 minutes or until the vegetables are wilted. Add the hot sauce, bay leaves, file powder, cayenne, thyme, oregano, basil, parsley, garlic, salt, and pepper and cook for 5 minutes. Add the roux, vegetable broth, and the reserved greens-cooking water, stirring well to blend in the roux. Bring to a boil, and then reduce the heat and simmer, uncovered, for 15 minutes. Add the cooked collard greens, okra, kidney beans, and rice and cook for 5 minutes. Remove the bay leaves and serve warm.

Makes 4 to 6 servings

SANDWICHES & ENTREES

.... *Grilled Fajitas Skewers*.....

Protein-Packed Onion Veggie Burgers

1 lb. firm tofu, mashed well
1 large onion, minced
4 Tbsp. wheat germ
4 Tbsp. unbleached all purpose flour
4 Tbsp. garlic powder
2 Tbsp. soy sauce
Salt & pepper, to taste
Oil for frying

Mix all the ingredients except oil in a bowl and form into patties. Heat some oil in a skillet and fry the patties until very brown and crisp. You can also form and freeze for quick use. Serve these burgers on buns or as patties with a sauce.

Makes 4 patties

Portobello Wrap

Portobello mushrooms
1 Tbsp. Paprika
1 Onion, fine minced
Garlic, diced
4 tomato-basil wraps
8 oz. hummus
8 oz. vegan pepper-jack cheese
baby spinach leaves
tomatoes, diced
onions, diced

Lightly sprinkle the Portobello mushrooms with the paprika, minced onions, and garlic. Place the mushrooms on a very hot grill and cook them, gill side up, for 3 minutes. Then turn them over and cook them for 3 minutes on the other side. Place the tomato-basil wraps flat on a dish. On each wrap, spread a thin layer of hummus topped lightly with vegan pepper-jack cheese. Add a few washed baby spinach leaves on top of the cheese. Sprinkle the diced tomatoes and onions over the spinach, followed by slices of the grilled mushrooms. Fold up flaps at opposite ends of each wrap and roll up gently, bake for 5 to 8 minutes at 350°F until wrap is just slightly brown, remove, cool a bit, and enjoy.

Makes 4 servings

Shepherd's Pie

4 medium potatoes, diced
2 Tbsp. vegan margarine
¼ cup soy milk
Salt and pepper, to taste
1 medium onion, finely chopped
1 Tbsp. olive oil
16 oz. vegan TVP pre-soaked (ground beef-style crumbles)
1 - 10.5oz. can mushroom gravy
1 - 6oz. can mixed peas and carrots, drained
Salt, garlic powder, pepper, and cayenne, to taste

Boil the potatoes for 20 minutes, or until tender. Drain and mash with the margarine and soy milk. Season with salt and pepper. In a medium pan, sauté the onion in the oil until translucent. In a medium bowl, mix the cooked onions, beef crumbles, mushroom gravy, peas and carrots, and spices. Pour into a pie pan. Top the crumble mixture with the potatoes, spreading to the edges. Bake in a 350°F oven for 30 to 40 minutes, until the potatoes are browned and the crumble mixture bubbles out the edges.

Makes 6 to 9 servings

Southwest Veggie Black Bean and Grain Burger

½ cup minced yellow onion

½ cup fresh or frozen corn,
thawed and well drained

¼ cup finely diced red bell pepper

¼ cup finely diced celery

2 tsp. minced garlic

4 Tbsp. olive oil

1 Tbsp. tomato paste mixed with 2 oz. water

¼ tsp. chipotle chili powder

1 tsp. mild chili powder

1 tsp. ground cumin

½ tsp. Celtic Sea Salt

4 oz. tempeh, finely diced

¼ cup tamari

1 cup black, red, or pinto beans, cooked, cooled, and lightly mashed (you can also use a combination of beans)

4 oz. soft tofu, well drained and crumbled

½ cup cooked millet, chilled

½ cup cooked wild rice blend or short grain brown rice, drained and chilled

1 ¼ cup cornmeal

¼ cup oat flour

Sauté the vegetables and garlic in the olive oil until soft. Add the tomato paste and seasonings. Set aside. Marinate the tempeh in tamari for 10 minutes. Drain. Sauté until golden. Place the vegetable mixture in a large bowl and add the tempeh, beans, tofu, millet, rice, ¼ cup cornmeal, and oat flour. Stir well. Shape the mixture into patties and press into a 3 ½-inch lid or metal burger-form lined with plastic wrap. Each burger should weigh approximately 5 oz. Remove from the form and dust with the remaining 1 cup of cornmeal. Place the burgers on a plate and freeze until firm. Heat a nonstick pan over medium heat and brush with coconut oil. Heat the burgers until golden brown, about 2 minutes on each side.

Makes 7 servings

✳ Enchilada Bake

1lb vegetarian burger crumbles

4 Tbsp taco seasoning

2 - 15oz. cans enchilada sauce

18 corn tortillas

2 - 15oz. cans pinto beans, drained

2 green onions, chopped

2 cups vegan cheddar cheese, shredded

1 - 4.5oz. can diced green chilies

2 cups corn chips, finely crushed

Preheat the oven to 375°F. In a small bowl, combine the burger crumbles and taco seasoning and set aside. Spray a 9-inch by 13-inch pan with oil. In layers, spread a generous amount of enchilada sauce, 6 corn tortillas, 2 cans of pinto beans, a handful of green onion, a third of the shredded cheese, half the can of green chilies, more enchilada sauce, 6 more tortillas, all the seasoned burger crumbles, another third of the cheese, the remaining green chilies, more enchilada sauce, then the final 6 tortillas, more enchilada sauce, and the rest of the cheese. Cover in foil and bake for 30 minutes. Remove the foil, top the entire casserole with the corn chips, and bake for another 15 to 30 minutes or until bubbly and browned.

Makes 6 servings

Singapore Street Noodles

Chewy rice sticks are topped with faux chicken and crisp veggies in this "taste of Asia."

2 gal. water
1 lb. package rice sticks
(available at Asian markets)
4 Tbsp. canola oil
8 oz. faux "shrimp" and
8 oz. diced faux "chicken"
or 1 lb. extra firm tofu pressed dry, diced
1 Tbsp. garlic, chopped
1 cup cabbage, julienned
½ cup carrots, julienned
2 medium tomatoes, diced
1 cup Singapore Sauce
1 bunch scallions (just the green part), cut into 2-in. pieces
¼ bunch cilantro, coarsely chopped
1 tsp. sesame oil
⅓ cup fried shallots
(optional, available at Asian markets)
1 lime, quartered

Bring water to a rolling boil. Place rice sticks into boiling water for 2 minutes (just until soft), then drain into a colander. Immediately rinse under hot water for 1 minute. Drain well (the noodles should still be slightly warm). Toss with 2 Tbsp. of oil and set aside to air dry a little. In a hot wok stir-fry faux "shrimp" and faux "chicken" or tofu with 2 Tbsp. of oil until just done. Add garlic, cabbage, carrots, and tomatoes and stir-fry for 2 minutes. Add rice stick noodles and stir-fry for one minute. Add Singapore Sauce and stir-fry until all ingredients are well mixed. Add scallions, cilantro, and sesame oil and toss briefly. Sprinkle with fried shallots, then garnish with a lime wedge.

Singapore Sauce

Serve this spicy sauce with Singapore Street Noodles.

¼ cup curry powder
Pinch of turmeric (optional)
¼ cup light soy sauce
1 cup vegetarian oyster sauce
¼ cup chili sauce
¼ cup ketchup

Mix well until the powders are well dissolved.

Makes 4 servings

Shrimp Linguine

½ lb. linguine
¼ cup olive oil
4 cloves garlic, chopped coarsely
1 pkg. vegan shrimp
1 tsp. lemon juice
Dash salt or garlic salt
¼ cup chopped fresh parsley

Cook the pasta according to the package directions. In a saucepan, heat the olive oil on very low heat. Add the garlic and slowly sauté for 30 minutes. Cook the shrimp with the lemon and salt until lightly browned on both sides. Drain the pasta and transfer to a serving bowl. Add the vegan shrimp, the garlic oil, and the fresh parsley, and toss. Add a dash of fresh olive oil, if needed. Serve immediately. Makes 2 servings

Wild Mushroom Fricassee Over Grilled Corn Cakes

For the Corn Cakes:
12 cups water
4 cups yellow corn grits
2 tsp. sea salt

For the Fricassee:
1 ½ pounds assorted mushrooms (Portobello, shiitake, oyster, chanterelle), cleaned (shiitake stems should be discarded)
4 Tbsp. nondairy margarine
1 ½ cup faux chicken stock or vegetable stock
3 shallots, minced
2 cloves of garlic, minced
1 Tbsp onion powder
1 tsp. fresh thyme, chopped
Sea salt and freshly ground black pepper

In a large pan, bring the water to a boil. Slowly whisk in the corn grits and salt, stirring frequently for 20 to 25 minutes. Pour into a pan or onto the countertop. Spread with a cake knife to ¾-inch thickness. Cut into 2- to 2 ½-inch rounds or squares and refrigerate for at least 2 hours. Grill for 2 to 3 minutes on each side. Clean and chop the mushrooms to the desired size. Sauté until tender in margarine and set mushrooms aside. Bring the stock to a simmer in a saucepan over medium. Add the shallots and garlic and cook over medium heat until the shallots are tender. Add all the mushrooms to the pan, and the thyme & onion powder. Add the faux chicken stock, simmer, and reduce to make a nice saucy consistency. Taste and adjust with salt and pepper. Top each grilled corn cake with 1 to 2 oz. of the mushroom fricassee. Makes 8 servings

✴ Pan-Seared Eggplant 'Mozzarella' Bake

4 Tbsp. vegetable oil
5 eggplants, sliced lengthwise into ¼-inch slices
1 cup flour
2 cups marinara sauce
1 lb. shredded vegan mozzarella cheese

Heat the oil in a large skillet over medium heat. Dredge the eggplant slices in the flour, then fry in the oil until golden brown. Drain on paper towels. Place a thin layer of the marinara sauce in the bottom of a deep 9 x 12-inch baking pan. Add a layer of the eggplant slices. Bake for 20 minutes at 350 and then sprinkle with the vegan mozzarella then bake for another 10 minutes, or until browned. Cool slightly before cutting. Serve over linguine or your favorite vegetables. Makes 5 servings

✳ Chicken and Dumplings

For the Dumplings:
2 cups flour
1 Tbsp. baking powder
½ tsp. salt
½ stick (4 Tbsp.) vegan margarine
¾ cup soy milk

For the Soup:
4 Tbsp. vegan margarine
½ cup onion, chopped
½ cup celery, chopped
½ cup flour
½ tsp. celery salt
½ tsp. pepper
8 cups vegetable broth
2 medium carrots, diced
1 lb. vegan chicken, small pieces
1 bay leaf

Combine the dry ingredients for the dumplings in a bowl. Mix the margarine with the dry mixture until crumbly. Add the soy milk, stirring until moistened. Add more soy milk, as needed, if the mixture is too dry. Knead the dough for 30 seconds on a well-floured surface, then roll to ⅛-inch thickness and cut into ½-inch squares. Place the margarine, onion, and celery for the soup in a large saucepan and sauté until the vegetables are soft. Add the flour, salt, and pepper to make a thick paste. Slowly mix in the broth and bring to a boil. Add the carrots, faux chicken, and bay leaf. Add the dumpling squares, stirring gently. Reduce the heat and simmer for 20 minutes, stirring often. Serve hot.

Makes 6 to 8 servings

Crispy Fried Tofu With Pineapple Chutney

For the Chutney:
3 Tbsp. peanut oil
3 oz. minced red onions
1 tsp. minced fresh garlic
1 tsp. minced fresh ginger
1 Tbsp. chopped fresh cilantro
2 lb. finely chopped fresh pineapple
¾ cup rice vinegar or apple cider
½ cup orange juice
¼ cup brown sugar
¼ tsp. ground cardamom
¼ tsp. crushed red pepper

For the Tofu:
2 ¼ cups unbleached flour
1 Tbsp. Chinese five-spice powder
12 oz. bread crumbs
4 Tbsp. sesame seeds
1 ½ cups soy milk
6 lbs. extra firm tofu, sliced into pieces ½"x2"x3"
In a large sauce pan, heat the oil over medium

heat. Add the onions, garlic, ginger, and cilantro. Sauté for 3 minutes. Add the pineapple & sauté 2 more minutes. Add the remaining chutney ingredients. Simmer 20 minutes, until thick and syrupy. Chill. Preheat fryer to 375°F. Combine the flour and five-spice powder in a bowl and set aside. Combine the bread crumbs and sesame seeds in a bowl. Set aside. Pour the soy milk into a small bowl. Dredge the tofu in the flour and dip into the soy milk. Press the tofu into the bread crumbs. Shake off excess crumbs. Immediately fry the tofu in the fryer for 2-3 minutes or until golden brown. Serve immediately with the pineapple chutney.

Makes 24 servings

Multi Mushroom Burger Patties

½ lb. shredded Portobello mushrooms
with gills removed
½ lb. shredded crimini mushrooms
¼ lb. shredded shiitake mushrooms
with stems removed
¼ lb. red bell pepper, seeded, minced,
and strained
½ lb. minced, strained yellow onions
⅛ cup minced garlic
¼ cup parsley, washed and chopped
Salt and pepper, to taste
¼ lb. falafel mix, dry
1 cup cooked oatmeal

Clean mushrooms, make sure they are completely dry then shred. Sauté bell peppers, onions, and garlic in canola oil until soft and most of the moisture evaporates out, at least 10 minutes. Add parsley. Add mushrooms and sauté until soft, allowing more moisture to evaporate out. Season to taste. Allow to cool on a flat baking pan. Mix well with falafel and oatmeal. Use a 4-oz. scoop to form patties. Place patties on a flat baking pan. Bake in a convection oven at 350°F for 15 minutes. Check for firmness and moisture content—they may need an additional 5 to 10 minutes. Let cool. Wrap individual patties in plastic wrap and place in an appropriate storage container.

Makes 8 patties

Sesame Tofu With Asparagus

¼ cup soy sauce
1 Tbsp. Dijon mustard
2 tsp. sesame oil
2 tsp. apple cider
2 Tbsp. minced chives
12 stalks asparagus
½ cup toasted sesame seeds
1 lb. extra-firm tofu, cut into ¼-inch slices
Oil cooking spray

In a small bowl, whisk together the 2 Tbsp. soy sauce, mustard, sesame oil, apple cider, and chives to form a vinaigrette. Steam the asparagus until the desired tenderness is reached (3 to 5 minutes), and drain. Toss in the vinaigrette to coat, and set aside. Place the sesame seeds in a bowl and dip each tofu piece into the seeds, covering all sides. Coat a large nonstick frying pan with the cooking spray and heat on medium. Arrange the tofu pieces in the pan, add the ¼ cup of soy sauce, and cook until golden brown on all sides. Sprinkle with half of the sesame seeds, then flip the tofu and sprinkle with the remaining sesame seeds. Cook for 1 minute. Serve the tofu and asparagus over rice.

Makes 4 servings

Philadelphia Cheese Steak Sandwiches

2 medium eggplants (about 1 pound) peel and
slice crosswise into ½-inch slices
Olive oil
Salt and pepper
Dried basil
3 cups sliced onions
1 Tbsp. soy sauce
2 Tbsp. water
1 tsp. dried basil
4 6-inch sub rolls
8 slices vegan cheddar cheese

Preheat the broiler or grill. Lightly oil a baking sheet. Place the eggplant slices on the sheet. Lightly brush each slice with olive oil. Sprinkle with salt, pepper, and basil.. Turn the slices over and repeat on the other side. Broil or grill the eggplant for 5 to 7 minutes on each side, or until nicely browned. While the eggplant is cooking, heat a large nonstick skillet over medium heat. Add the onions, soy sauce, water, and basil. Mix well, breaking the onion slices into rings. Cook for 10 minutes, or until the onions are translucent. Stir several times while cooking. To serve, place the eggplant in the rolls, slightly overlapping the slices. Top with the onions and cheese slices. Melt in oven for a minute

Makes 4 servings

Soy Chicken-and-Beef With Pineapple

Mark's Favorite Tricks of the Trade

For the Soy Chicken and Beef:
1 ¼ cups firm tofu
½ cup boiled shitake mushroom stems
3 Tbsp. cornstarch
½ tsp. salt
½ tsp. sugar
½ tsp. white pepper
1 tsp. Chinese five-spice powder
¼ tsp. baking powder
1 ½ tsp. dark soy sauce

Put all the ingredients, except for the dark soy sauce, into a blender or food processor and blend coarsely. Remove ½ from the blender and set aside to use for the "chicken." For the "beef," add the dark soy sauce to the blender and blend until well combined. Wrap each tightly with cheesecloth and steam for 20 minutes. Slice and then brown in a skillet with a little oil. Set aside.

For the Stir-Fry:
2 Tbsp. cold water
2 tsp. apple cider
1 ½ tsp. sugar
1 ½ tsp. ketchup
1 tsp. soy sauce
½ medium green bell pepper, sliced
½ medium red bell pepper, sliced
½ medium pineapple, sliced

Combine the water, cider, sugar, ketchup, and soy sauce in a wok or frying pan and heat on high. Add the "chicken" and "beef" and stir-fry until covered with the sauce. Add the peppers and pineapple and stir-fry for about 3 minutes, being careful not to overcook. Serve immediately.

Makes 4 servings

Vegan Sloppy Joes

2 Tbsp. vegetable oil
1 large onion, diced
2 medium green peppers, seeded and diced
1 ½ cups boiling water
2 ½ cups tomato sauce
1 Tbsp. chili powder
1 Tbsp onion powder
1 tsp. salt
3 Tbsp. BBQ spice
1 Tbsp. mustard
1 Tbsp. sugar
1 ½ cups dry TVP (textured vegetable protein)

Sauté the onion and the green peppers in oil until the onions are translucent. Add the remaining ingredients and simmer for 20 minutes. Serve on buns.

Makes 4 to 6 servings

Sloppy Joes #2

1 Tbsp. olive oil
½ cup minced onion
½ cup minced green bell pepper
1 lb. pre soaked TVP drained
6 Tbsp. ketchup
6 Tbsp. chili sauce
½ tsp. salt
1 tsp sugar
2 tsp BBQ spice
Pepper to taste
4 burger buns, lightly toasted

Add onion and green pepper and olive oil, and sautè until the vegetables are well cooked, about 5 minutes. Add the TVP and sautè for another 5 minutes. Add the remaining ingredients and continue to cook over medium heat until the mixture is heated through. Add a little water if the mixture is too dry. Spoon onto lightly toasted burger buns.

Makes 4 servings

Egg-less Salad Sandwiches

8 oz. firm tofu, drained and diced or mash
¼ red bell pepper, finely chopped
1 small carrot, finely shredded
2 scallions, finely chopped
2 Tbsp. vegan mayonnaise
1 Tbsp. chopped fresh parsley
1 tsp. yellow mustard
1 Tbsp. finely chopped dill pickle
¼ tsp. salt
⅛ tsp. pepper

Combine all the ingredients in a medium-size bowl, mixing well.

Makes 4 sandwiches

Eggless Salad #2

Soft tofu is the perfect substitute for eggs in this perfectly seasoned vegan delight.

2 Tbsp. Vegan mayonnaise
1 tsp. distilled vinegar (optional)
1 tsp. mustard
1 tsp. sugar
½ tsp. ground turmeric
1 Tbsp. dried parsley
1 lb. tofu
1 Tbsp. onion powder
2 Tbsp. celery powder
Salt and pepper, to taste
Add fine chopped celery, onion and red pepper to really kick it up.

Mix together the mayonnaise, vinegar, mustard, sugar, turmeric, and parsley to make the dressing. Place in the refrigerator until chilled. Stir in onion and celery powder. Crumble the tofu and add to the dressing. Add fine chopped celery, onion and red pepper. Salt and pepper to taste and chill for several hours before serving.

Makes 4 servings

Mac & Cheese Casserole

3 ½ cups elbow macaroni
½ cup vegan margarine
½ cup flour
3 ½ cups boiling water
1 Tbsp. salt
1 tsp. sugar
1 ½ tsp. garlic powder
1 ½ tsp. onion powder
Pinch of turmeric
¼ cup vegetable oil
1 cup nutritional yeast flakes
Paprika, to taste

Preheat the oven to 350°F. Cook the elbow macaroni according to the package directions. Drain and set aside. In a saucepan, melt margarine over low heat. Whisk in the flour. Continue whisking over medium heat until smooth and bubbly. Whisk in the boiling water, salt, soy sauce, garlic powder, onion powder and turmeric. Continue whisking until dissolved. Once thick and bubbling, whisk in the oil and the nutritional yeast flakes. Mix ¾ of the sauce with the noodles and place in a casserole dish. Cover with the remaining sauce and sprinkle with the paprika. Bake for 15 minutes. Broil for a few minutes until crisp.

Makes 5 servings

Vegan Mac & Cheese #2

1 lb. macaroni pasta
½ tub vegan sour cream
3 Tbsp. water
½ cup nutritional yeast
½ cup tahini
1 Tbsp. light miso (optional)
½ tsp. garlic powder
½ tsp. salt
½ tsp. onion powder
½ tsp. paprika

Boil the macaroni until it is soft.
Mix all the other ingredients in a large bowl, add the pasta, and enjoy! You can also top with bread crumbs and brown in the oven if you like.

Makes 4 to 6 servings

Roasted Tempeh With a Creamy Dijon Sauce

For the Tempeh:

1 lb. tempeh cut into 4 portions
2 ½ cups vegetable stock
¾ cup wheat-free tamari
¼ cup apple cider
2 bay leaves
2 Tbsp. finely chopped fresh rosemary
3 garlic cloves, minced

Bring a medium pot of water to a boil and drop in the tempeh. Cook for about 10 minutes. (Tempeh has a mildly bitter flavor that boiling will remove.) Meanwhile, mix together the vegetable stock, tamari, apple cider, bay leaves, rosemary, and garlic. Place the tempeh in a baking pan and pour the liquid mixture on top. Bake, uncovered, for 30 to 40 minutes in a 350°F oven, turning once halfway through. Remove from the oven but leave the tempeh in the pan to soak up the remainder of the liquid while it cools to ensure moist tempeh. After the liquid is absorbed, reheat in the oven until slightly browned on the edges, about 10 minutes or less.

For the Dijon Sauce:

½ cup grainy Dijon mustard
½ cup apple cider
¼ cup soy milk
2 Tbsp. maple syrup
2 Tbsp. brown rice syrup
1 tsp. orange zest

Mix together all the ingredients in a small saucepan over medium heat and bring to a simmer. Cook for 20 minutes, until slightly thickened, stirring frequently. Pour over the tempeh.

Grilled Fajitas Skewers

Juice of 2 limes
2 Tbsp. olive oil
1 clove garlic, minced
1 jalapeño pepper, seeded and minced
2 Tbsp. minced fresh cilantro
1 Tbsp. chili powder
¼ tsp. cayenne pepper
1 tsp. salt
1 lb. extra-firm tofu, cut into 1-inch strips
2 ears fresh corn
1 large red onion
1 red bell pepper, cut into ½ inch slivers
1 green bell pepper, cut into ½ inch slivers
12 cherry tomatoes
4 large flour tortillas
Guacamole & salsa

Put the lime juice, olive oil, garlic, jalapeño pepper, cilantro, chili powder, salt and cayenne pepper in a jar with a tight-fitting lid and shake well. Put the tofu in a shallow pan, add the lime juice mixture, and marinate in the refrigerator, stirring occasionally, for several hours. Meanwhile, remove the husks from the corn and soak it in cold water for 1 hour. Drain the corn and wrap it in aluminum foil. Grill for 20 to 30 minutes, turning often, until the corn is lightly charred. Cut the corn kernels off the cob. Parboil the onion and cut into quarters. Thread the onion, bell peppers, and tomatoes onto skewers and brush with some of the lime marinade. Grill, turning often, until lightly charred. Place the tofu on the grill, cover with a lid or aluminum foil and cook, basting occasionally with the marinade until the tofu is light brown. Heat each tortilla briefly on the grill. Divide the vegetables and tofu equally among the tortillas, and then roll them up fajita-style. Serve with guacamole and salsa.

Makes 4 servings

Vegan Lemon Chicken

2 Tbsp. olive oil
1 lb. vegan chicken strips, chopped
1 lb. button mushrooms, sliced
6 fresh large basil leaves, thinly sliced
1 lemon, sliced into wedges
2 Tbsp. chopped chives
¼ cup vegetable stock
1 cup tomato sauce
Salt and pepper, to taste

Heat the oil in a large pan over medium heat. Add the "chicken," mushrooms, basil, lemon, and chives. Sauté for 5 minutes. Add the tomato sauce and vegetable stock. Simmer, covered, over medium-low heat for 20 minutes, or until thickened, stirring occasionally. Taste and season with salt and pepper. Serve over rice or pasta.

Makes 4 to 6 servings

Healthy Vegetable Wraps

4 Tbsp. vegan cream cheese
4 10-inch flour tortillas
1 cup shredded spinach
¼ cup alfalfa sprouts
½ cup shredded red cabbage
½ cup sliced avocado
¼ cup chopped tomatoes
½ cup diced cucumbers
2 Tbsp. finely diced red onion
Salt and pepper, to taste

Spread one tablespoon of cream cheese over each tortilla. Sprinkle an even amount of the remaining ingredients on each wrap; roll up. And now the fun part, Splash with BBQ sauce for a BBQ Wrap, Asian Sauces for Asian Wrap, Pesto sauces for an Italian Wrap, Salsa for a Mexican Wrap.

Makes 4 servings.

Lentil Loaf

1 ½ cups lentils, rinsed
3 ½ cups water
1 onion, diced
½ cup red pepper, diced fine
¼ cup vegetable oil
2 cups cooked rice
2 tsp. garlic powder
1 tsp. salt
¼ cup ketchup or barbecue sauce, plus more for spreading on the loaf
1 tsp. sage
½ tsp. marjoram

Place the lentils and the water in a large pan and cook over medium heat until tender. Meanwhile, in a frying pan, cook the onions in the oil over medium-high heat. Partially mash the lentils and stir in the onions, rice, garlic powder, salt, ketchup, sage, and marjoram. Press into an oiled loaf pan and spread some ketchup on top. Bake at 350°F for 1 hour.

Makes 4 to 6 servings

Indonesian Tofu Stir-Fry

For the Indonesian Sauce:
1 ½ cups tamari
½ cup agave nectar
1 cup fresh lime juice
1 cup veggie broth
2 Tbsp. freshly grated ginger
2 Tbsp. freshly chopped garlic
1 tsp. cayenne pepper
1 cup smooth peanut butter
Water to give it a smooth, sauce-like consistency

Combine all the ingredients for the sauce in a blender. Add the water and blend until smooth.

To Assemble:
2 Tbsp. olive oil
1 block tofu, pressed and cubed
Vegetables of your choice

Heat the olive oil in a large pan. Sauté the tofu and vegetables. Add enough of the Indonesian sauce to cover. Cook until reduced and thickened. Serve over rice or tossed with soba noodles.

Makes 4 to 6 servings

Portobello Mushroom

8 Tbsp. (1 stick) vegan margarine
2 large Portobello mushrooms
2 Tbsp. vegetarian Worcestershire sauce
4 cloves garlic, finely chopped
¼ cup pine or soy nuts
2 small red or yellow bell peppers, chopped
1 small zucchini chopped
½ cup fresh peas
1 cup sprouts
1 Tbsp. finely chopped basil
¼ tsp. salt
1 tsp. white pepper
Pinch cayenne pepper

For the sauce:
⅓ cup chopped shallots or onions
1 cup soy milk
½ cup dry white wine or vegetable broth
¼ cup orange juice
1 tsp. grated orange peel

Preheat the oven to 375 degrees. In a large skillet, melt 2 Tbsp. of the margarine over medium heat and cook the mushrooms with the Worcestershire sauce for 4 minutes, turning once. Remove the mushrooms and arrange them on a baking sheet gill side up. In the same skillet, melt 2 more Tbsp. margarine over medium-high heat and brown the garlic and nuts. Add the bell peppers and cook 4 minutes, stirring occasionally, until almost tender. Stir in the remaining vegetables, basil, salt, white pepper and cayenne pepper. Evenly spoon the vegetable mixture onto the mushrooms. Bake 10 minutes. For the sauce, melt the remaining margarine over medium heat and cook the shallots for 4 minutes, stirring occasionally, until just golden. Stir in the soy milk, wine, orange juice and orange peel. Bring to a boil over high heat. Reduce heat to medium and continue boiling, stirring occasionally, until the mixture thickens, about 3 minutes. Strain. To serve, spoon the sauce over the mushrooms.

Makes 2 servings.

Tofu-Spinach Lasagna

½ lb. lasagna noodles
2 - 10oz. packages frozen chopped spinach,
thawed and drained
1 lb. soft tofu
1 lb. firm tofu
1 Tbsp. sugar
¼ cup soy milk
1 tsp. garlic powder
2 Tbsp. lemon juice
3 tsp. minced fresh basil
2 tsp. salt
4 cups tomato sauce

Cook the lasagna noodles according to the package directions. Drain and set aside. Preheat the oven to 350 degrees. Squeeze the spinach as dry as possible and set aside. Place the tofu, sugar, soy milk, garlic powder, lemon juice, basil, and salt in a food processor or blender and blend until smooth. Stir in the spinach. Cover the bottom of a 9-inch-by-13-inch baking dish with a thin layer of tomato sauce, then a layer of noodles (use about one-third of the noodles). Follow with half of the tofu filling. Continue in the same order, using half of the remaining tomato sauce and noodles and all of the remaining tofu filling. End with the remaining noodles, covered by the remaining tomato sauce. Bake for 25 to 30 minutes.

Makes 6 to 8 servings

Baked Stuffed Zucchini

2 zucchinis, cut in half lengthwise
1 small onion, finely chopped
4 Tbsp. tomato sauce
½ tsp. parsley
1 clove garlic, chopped
2 Tbsp. matzo meal
Salt and pepper to taste

Scoop out the pulp of the zucchini halves. Sauté the pulp, onion, tomato sauce, parsley, and garlic in a pan for 5 minutes. Add the matzo meal to the mixture and mix well. Stuff the zucchini with the mixture. Place in baking dish with a little water on the bottom. Bake at 375 degrees for 30 minutes or until the zucchini shells are soft.

Makes 4-6 servings

Bold Beef Stroganoff

1-lb. bag egg-free pasta
½ cup onion, chopped
1 Tbsp. vegetable oil
1-lb. pkg. burger crumbles
1 - 10oz. can mushroom gravy
2 - 5oz. cans sliced mushrooms, drained
⅛ tsp. garlic powder
¼ tsp. pepper
⅛ tsp. salt
½ cup vegan sour cream
¼ cup burgundy cooking wine (optional)

Cook the pasta in boiling water until the desired tenderness is reached. In a large skillet, brown the onion in the oil. Whip the sour cream with a splash of water until smooth, this gives you a smooth product instead of having those little white lumps that make it look curdled. Add the remaining ingredients, stir, and cook over medium heat for 15 minutes. Drain the pasta, and serve the sauce over the noodles.

Makes 4 servings

Garlic-Ginger Tofu Stir-Fry

1 tsp. minced ginger
1 garlic clove, minced
1 Tbsp. olive oil
3 Tbsp. soy sauce
¼ cup water
1 Tbsp. arrowroot powder or cornstarch
2 Tbsp. vegetable oil
1 16-oz. pkg. firm tofu, drained and cut into
1x½-inch pieces
1 tsp. soy sauce
2 carrots, cut into 2-inch strips
1 red pepper, sliced
1 large bok choy cut into ½-inch pieces
½ medium onion, sliced
½ cup yellow squash, sliced into ½-inch pieces
Cooked lo mien or soba noodles

Sauté the ginger, and garlic in the olive oil for 2 minutes over medium heat. Add the soy sauce and water, stirring until well combined. Stir in the cornstarch and simmer over low heat until the tofu and vegetables are ready. Heat the vegetable oil over medium-high heat in a nonstick 12-inch skillet. Add the tofu and cook, stirring frequently until heated through and browned on all sides, about 10 to 15 minutes. Add the soy sauce and stir-fry for 1 minute. Transfer to a bowl. Then stir-fry the carrots, red pepper, bok choy, onions, and squash to the skillet and stir-fry until the vegetables are tender but crisp, about 3 minutes. Add the prepared sauce and tofu and stir-fry until all the ingredients are coated and heated, about 2 minutes. Serve immediately over lo mien.

Spinach-Tofu Manicotti

1 pkg. large manicotti tubes
1 lb. tofu, drained and rinsed
1 - 10oz. box frozen spinach, thawed and squeezed dry
1 Tbsp. Italian seasoning (blend of oregano, marjoram, thyme, rosemary, basil, sage)
½ tsp. salt
3 green onions, sliced thin
8 oz. white button mushrooms, coarsely chopped
32 oz. of your favorite marinara pasta sauce

Boil 10 manicotti shells until they're just shy of al dente and drain them. Plop the tofu into a medium-sized mixing bowl and crumble with your hands. Add the spinach and fold into the tofu with a fork, breaking up the strands of spinach, and mix evenly with the crumbled tofu. Stir in Italian seasoning, salt, onions, and mushrooms. Using your fingers, stuff the manicotti shells with the tofu mixture until each is plump and full. Lay them in a covered casserole dish and pour your favorite tomato-based pasta sauce over them. Cover and bake at 350 degrees for 45 minutes to an hour. Remove from the oven and give it a few minutes to cool off before serving.

Vegan Cheeseburger Macaroni

3 ½ cups macaroni noodles (uncooked)
½ cup vegan margarine
½ cup flour
3 ½ cups boiling water
1 tsp. salt 2 Tbsp. soy sauce
1 Tbsp. garlic powder
1Tbsp. onion powder
Pinch turmeric
¼ cup oil
1 cup nutritional yeast flakes
1 lb burger crumbles
Paprika, as desired

Cook the macaroni and set it aside. In a saucepan, melt the margarine over low heat. Mix in the flour with a whisk and continue whisking over a medium flame until the mixture is smooth and bubbly. Stir in the boiling water, salt, soy sauce, garlic & onion powder, and turmeric. Stir well to dissolve the flour mixture and cook until it thickens and bubbles. Add the oil and nutritional yeast. Heat the Boca crumbles in a frying pan. Mix part of the sauce with the noodles, put in a casserole dish and pour a generous amount of sauce on top, mixing together and adding Boca crumbles. Sprinkle with paprika and bake for 15 minutes at 350 degrees.

Makes 4 servings

Barbecue Temphe

2 cups onion, cut in half moons
2 cups green pepper, slivers
2 cups red pepper, slivers
3 - 8 oz. pkgs. multigrain tempeh, cut into 1-inch cubes
2 Tbsp. olive oil
2 Tbsp. tamari
Your favorite BBQ sauce

Lightly oil a large baking dish. Place the sliced onions and peppers in the pan. Bake at 375 degrees for 20 minutes to slightly roast the vegetables. Remove the pan from the oven, transfer the vegetables to a plate, and set aside. Place the tempeh in the same baking pan. In a small bowl, whisk together the olive oil and tamari. Pour the tamari mixture over the tempeh. Bake the tempeh at 375 degrees for 15 minutes stirring once. Cook until the tempeh is lightly browned and the liquid is absorbed. Remove the pan from the oven. Add the reserved vegetables along with BBQ Sauce, and toss gently to combine. Return the pan to the oven, bake an additional 15 minutes, or until the sauce is bubbly. Serve as a main dish or side dish, or as a sandwich filling.

Serves 6-8

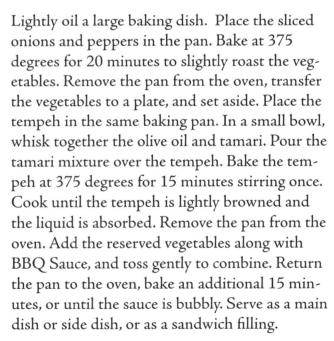

Papa's Mock Meatloaf

1 medium onion, diced
½ green pepper, diced
3 Tbsp. olive oil
2 lb soaked weight beef TVP
¼ cup oatmeal, dry
2 slices white bread, crumbled
3 Tbsp. ketchup
2 tsp. garlic salt
1 tsp. pepper

Coating ingredients:
¼ cup ketchup
¼ cup brown sugar
½ tsp. dry mustard
½ tsp. nutmeg

Sauté the onion and green pepper in the oil over medium heat until soft. Combine in a bowl with the ground beef alternative, oatmeal, bread, ketchup, garlic salt, and pepper. Thoroughly mix with a spoon or your hands. Press the mixture into an oiled loaf pan. Cover with foil and bake at 375 degrees for 30 minutes. Meanwhile, mix together the ingredients for the coating and set aside. Remove the loaf from the oven and turn it out onto a baking sheet. Spread the coating over the entire loaf. Cook, uncovered, for another 15 minutes.

Makes 6 servings

Asparagus & Red Pepper Fritatta

Water
1 lb. asparagus, tough ends trimmed
safflower oil, for oiling pan
1 lb. firm tofu, crumbled
½ cup soy milk, rice milk, or other non-dairy milk of choice
2 Tbsp. arrowroot
2 Tbsp. nutritional yeast flakes
1 Tbsp. garlic, minced
1 ½ t. agar-agar flakes
1 tsp. Dijon mustard
1 tsp. sea salt
¼ tsp. turmeric
⅛ tsp. white pepper
¼ cup freshly chopped basil
¼ cup freshly chopped parsley
1 cup red pepper, fine diced
½ cup green onions, thinly sliced
½ cup vegan soy mozzarella cheese, shredded

Begin by preparing the asparagus: fill a medium saucepan half full with water, place it over high heat, and bring to a boil. Slice the asparagus spears diagonally into 1-inch pieces and place them in a fine mesh strainer. Place the strainer in the boiling water and cook the asparagus in the water for 2 minutes to blanch them. Remove the strainer from the water and set the asparagus aside. Lightly oil a 10-inch quiche pan or spring-form pan and set aside. In a food processor, place the tofu, soy milk, arrowroot, nutritional yeast flakes, garlic, agar-agar, Dijon mustard, salt, turmeric, and white pepper, and process for 2 minutes or until it forms a smooth puree. Pour half of the tofu mixture into the prepared quiche pan, evenly distribute the blanched asparagus and the remaining ingredients in the pan, and then top with the remaining tofu mixture. Using a spoon, slightly swirl the two mixtures together, and then smooth the top. Bake at 375 degrees for 35-45 minutes or until the filling is firm to the touch and dry on the top. Remove the frittata from the oven and allow to cool for 10 minutes before cutting. Serve warm, cold, or at room temperature.

Yield: One 10-inch frittata

Sesame Soy Chicken With Mixed Vegetable

1 cup dry chunky textured soy protein
2 cups sliced mixed vegetables:
Carrot
Snow peas
Bamboo shoots
Celery
Water chestnuts
1 Tbsp. olive oil
1 tsp. minced garlic
1 tsp. minced ginger

Condiment mix:

1 tbsp. soy sauce
1 tsp. sugar
⅛ tsp. salt
⅛ tsp. pepper
⅓ cup water
1 tsp. corn starch
Steamed broccoli floweret, blanched for garnish
Toasted sesame seeds

Soak chunky textured soy protein overnight. Drain. Blanch all the vegetables in boiling water for one minute, and then rinse in cold water. In a wok over high flame, add vegetable oil. Add garlic and ginger, cooking until light brown. Add blanched vegetable mix and textured soy protein. Stir-fry for about one minute, depending on desired tenderness. Add condiment mix; cook for 1 minute. Arrange broccoli around plate. Transfer sautéed vegetables to the middle of serving plate. Sprinkle with roasted sesame seeds and serve.

Seitan Piccatta

1 Tbsp. Egg Replacer
4 Tbsp. water
2 cups unbleached flour
1 tsp. salt
1 tsp. pepper
¼ tsp. oregano
6 medallions of seitan

For the sauce:

2 Tbsp. olive oil
2 Tbsp. unbleached flour
¼ cup diced onions
1 cup vegetable stock
¼ cup lemon juice
¼ cup capers
1 tsp. turmeric
2 cups water
1 tsp. sea salt
½ tsp. pepper

Mix egg replacer with water until dissolved. Mix the remaining ingredients together in a bowl, except for the seitan. Dip one seitan medallion at a time in the egg-replacer mixture, then coat it in the flour mixture. Heat 1 teaspoonful of oil in a sauté pan and cook the seitan until golden brown. Pour 2 tablespoonfuls of sauce on top of each medallion of seitan and serve with rice and roasted vegetables.

For the sauce: In a hot pan, heat olive oil and flour to make a roux. Let the roux cook for 5 minute stirring constantly, then add diced onions, vegetable stock, and lemon juice. Stir mixture then add the capers, turmeric, and water and stir until the turmeric is completely dissolved. Let this delectable sauce cook for 20 minutes over a low flame. Add sea salt and pepper. Keep hot on stove to pour over medallions of seitan.

Tropical Veggie Burgers

For the Veggie Burgers:
1 cup green lentils, rinsed
¼ cup brown rice
2 cups vegetable broth
Water sufficient to cover the lentils and rice
Salt, to taste
1 ½ Tbsp. vegan margarine
1 onion, chopped
⅓ cup shredded carrot
2 Tbsp. hot sauce
¾ cup panko
4 garlic cloves, minced
4 tsp. minced fresh ginger
½ tsp. ground allspice
1 tsp. cumin

Put the lentils and rice in a saucepan with the vegetable broth, adding enough water to cover by about 2 inches. Season with the salt and bring to a boil over high heat, then reduce the heat and simmer, uncovered, until the lentils and rice are tender, about 30 minutes. Drain any excess liquid and place the lentils and rice in a large bowl. Let cool completely. Meanwhile, melt the margarine in a skillet over medium heat and sauté the onion until tender, about 4 min-

utes. Cool slightly and then add to the lentils and rice. Stir in the remaining ingredients and season with the salt. Add a little bit of water if necessary to get the right consistency. Form into patties and place in the refrigerator for 30 minutes to 1 hour. Grill for 5 to 7 minutes on each side, until grill marks appear and the patties are hot.

To Assemble:
1 can pineapple rings, drained
1 red onion, thinly sliced
1 Tbsp. margarine
Kaiser rolls
Lettuce
Vegan mayonnaise

Grill the pineapple rings until caramelized, about 5 minutes on each side. Grill the onion until lightly browned. Spread the margarine over the rolls and grill until lightly browned. Place the veggie burgers on the buns and top with the pineapple, onions, lettuce, and vegan mayonnaise.

Makes 6 to 8 servings

Kentucky BBQ Sauce

½ cup tomato paste
½ cup cider vinegar
⅓ cup maple syrup
¼ cup tamari
1 T. olive oil
1 T. garlic, minced
1 T. ginger, minced
1 T. dry mustard
¼ t. pepper
¼ t. cayenne pepper

1 t. salt
Combine all ingredients in a food processor or blender and puree until smooth. Place in a sealed jar and keep refrigerated for up to 2 weeks.

Yield: 2 Cups

.....West Coast Soy-Sausage Lasagna

Mac and 'Cheese' Florentine

8 oz. elbow macaroni

10oz. pkg. frozen chopped spinach, well drained

2 Tbsp. olive oil

1 medium yellow onion, chopped

½ cup raw cashews

1 ¾ cups water

15.5oz. can white beans, drained and rinsed

¼ tsp. dry mustard

¼ tsp. cayenne pepper

Pinch of ground nutmeg

Salt, to taste

½ cup dry bread crumbs

Cook the macaroni in a pot of salted boiling water until al dente, about 8 minutes. Drain and place in a large bowl. Add the spinach and toss to combine. Set aside. Heat 1 Tbsp. of the oil in a medium-sized skillet over medium heat. Add the onion and cook, covered, until softened, about 5 minutes. Set aside. Grind the cashews to a powder in a blender or food processor. Add 1 cup of the water and blend until smooth. Add the onion, beans, miso paste, remaining ¾ cup water, lemon juice, mustard, cayenne, and nutmeg. Blend until smooth. Season with salt. Pour over the macaroni and spinach and mix well. Transfer to a lightly oiled slow cooker. Cover and cook on low for 3 hours. Close to serving time, heat the remaining 1 Tbsp. of oil in a small skillet over medium heat. Add the bread crumbs, stirring well to coat. Cook, stirring, until lightly toasted, about 3 to 4 minutes. Remove from the heat and set aside. When ready to serve, sprinkle the toasted crumbs on top of the casserole.

Makes 4 servings

West Coast Soy-Sausage Artichoke Lasagna

For the Tofu Ricotta filling:

1 lb. firm tofu, drained

1 Tbsp. lemon juice

2 tsp. dried basil

1 tsp. salt

½ tsp. fresh garlic, minced

Other Ingredients:

14oz. package of vegetarian soy sausage

2 Tbsp. olive oil

1 - 16oz. cans artichoke hearts, packed in water

12 oz of frozen spinach

1 lb of lasagna noodles

1 - 32oz. jar prepared tomato sauce

Mash all the ingredients for the tofu ricotta filling together and set aside. In a large pan, cook the soy sausage in the olive oil, breaking it up into crumbles. Drain the artichoke hearts, cut into quarters or smaller pieces, and set aside. Put the frozen spinach in a colander and drain. Set aside. Cook the lasagna noodles according to the instructions on the package. Cover the bottom of your lasagna pan with some tomato sauce. Put down a layer of pasta. Put half of the tofu mixture over the noodles, followed by half each of the soy sausage, artichoke hearts, and spinach. Repeat layering until all the ingredients are gone, ending with the pasta and sauce. Cover with aluminum foil and bake for 1 hour at 350°F. Before cutting and serving, let sit for 15 minutes to allow the pasta to settle. Makes 6 to 9 servings

Green Gumbo

2 Quarts water
1 lb. collard greens, washed well, roughly chopped (or 1 - 10 oz. pkg. frozen)
1 lb. turnip greens, washed well, roughly chopped (or 1 - 10 oz. pkg. frozen)
1 lb. kale, washed well, roughly chopped (or 1 - 10 oz. pkg. frozen)
1 lb. spinach, washed well, roughly chopped (or 1 - 10 oz. pkg. frozen)
¼ cup olive oil
¼ cup unbleached flour
1 ½ cups onion, diced
1 cup celery, diced
1 cup green pepper, diced
2 Tbsp. garlic, minced
3 cups cabbage, shredded
3 Tbsp. Cajun Seasoning
½ t. salt
1 bay leaf
4 cups water
2 cups brown rice, rinsed
¼ cup freshly chopped parsley
¼ cup nutritional yeast flakes
Dash Green Chili Pepper Sauce

In a large saucepan, place the 2 Quarts of water, and bring to a boil. Cook the collard greens in the boiling water for 2-3 minutes to blanch them. Using a slotted spoon, remove the collard greens from the boiling water, place them in a large bowl, and set aside. Cook the turnip greens, kale, and spinach in the same manner, and add to the bowl of collard greens. If using frozen greens, cook them individually in the boiling water until thawed, then remove them with a slotted spoon, and place them in a bowl for later use. Set the liquid aside for use in the gumbo. In a large pot, stir together the oil and flour to form a roux. Cook the roux over medium heat, while stirring constantly for 20 minutes, or until it is a golden (nutty) color. Add the onion, celery, green pepper, and garlic, stir well to combine, and cook an additional 5 minutes or until the vegetables are soft. Slowly, stir a little of the greens' cooking liquid into the roux-vegetable mixture, blending them thoroughly together, and then stir in the remaining cooking liquid. Add the reserved greens, cabbage, Cajun seasoning, salt, and bay leaf, and bring to a boil. Cover, reduce the heat to low, and simmer for 45 minutes. Cook rice as directed. After the gumbo has simmered for 45 minutes, add the parsley and nutritional yeast, and simmer an additional 5 minutes. Taste and add additional Cajun seasoning or salt, if needed. Serve the gumbo in bowls over the brown rice.

Serves 8

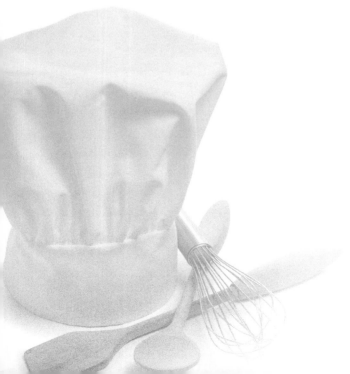

Seitan Stroganoff Over Eggless Noodles

For the Stroganoff:
⅓ lb. vegan margarine
⅔ cup all-purpose flour
½ cup olive oil
5 lbs. prepared seitan, drained and cut into 1-inch cubes
1 ½ lbs. onion, chopped
3 lbs. white mushrooms, sliced
1 ½ Tbsp. chopped garlic
3 ½ qts. vegetable stock
3 bay leaves
1 Tbsp. dried thyme
2 Tbsp. vegan browning seasoning
Salt and pepper, to taste

Melt the margarine in a large saucepan. Add the flour and cook for 5 minutes to form a roux. Set aside. Heat the oil in a medium saucepot. Add the seitan cubes and cook for 7 minutes, or until browned. Add the onions and sauté for 5 minutes, or until just soft. Add the mushrooms and cook for 5 minutes, or until mostly cooked through. Add the garlic and sauté for an addi-tional 3 minutes. Place the vegetable stock, bay leaves, and thyme in the pot and simmer for 15 minutes. While the liquid is simmering, whisk in the prepared roux (a little bit at a time to get the thickness you want), bring back to a slow simmer, and cook for 10 minutes. Season with the browning sauce, salt, and pepper.

For the Noodles:
3 lbs. eggless flat noodles
¼ cup margarine
Place the noodles in rapidly boiling salted water and cook for 2 minutes less than the package directions specify. Drain and toss with the margarine.

To Assemble:
1 qt. vegan sour cream
⅓ cup chopped chives

Serve the stroganoff over the noodles and gar-nish with the vegan sour cream and the chives.

Makes 25 6-oz. servings

Mediterranean Beef Kebabs With Green Olive Relish

For the Kebabs:
1 lb Vegan Steak Strips
3 Tbsp. olive oil
 steak seasoning, to taste
1 red pepper, cut into 1-inch squares
1 yellow zucchini, sliced into thick rounds
1 red onion, cut into 1-inch chunks
1 dozen Button Mushrooms
16 dried apricots
6-8 skewers

Preheat a grill or broiler to medium-high. Toss the "steak" strips in the olive oil and flavor with the seasoning. Soak skewers and alternating the steak strips, red pepper, zucchini, red onion, and apricots with the button mushrooms on the end. Broil or grill for 2 to 4 minutes per side.

For the Relish:
1 medium tomato, finely diced
¼ cup chopped green olives
2 Tbsp. capers, rinsed dry and chopped
2 Tbsp. olive oil
Zest and juice of 1 lemon
1 tsp. minced fresh garlic
¼ cup chopped fresh basil
Salt and pepper, and pinch of sugar to taste

In a medium bowl, combine all the ingredients. Serve with the kebabs.

Makes 6 to 8 servings

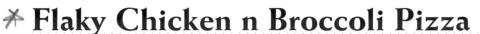

Flaky Chicken n Broccoli Pizza

1 container vegan crescent rolls
½ cup chopped vegan chicken
6 cherry tomatoes, sliced
1 cup chopped broccoli blanched
2 Tbsp. extra virgin olive oil
¼ tsp. red pepper flakes or more, to taste
¼ cup vegan shredded cheese of choice
Sea salt, to taste

Preheat the oven to 400°F. Roll the dough out on a lightly greased cookie sheet. Gently press the crescent roll breaks together to form a single crust. Spread the vegan chicken, tomatoes, and broccoli across the dough. Sprinkle with the olive oil, red pepper flakes, cheese and salt. Bake for 10 to 12 minutes, or until the dough is golden brown.

Makes 2 to 3 servings

Roasted Veggie Pita Bread Pizza

½ cup vegan shredded cheese
1 red onion, cut into small wedges
1 red pepper, thinly sliced
1 yellow pepper, thinly sliced
sliced mushrooms
1 Tbsp. olive oil
1 Tbsp. balsamic vinegar (optional)
½ tsp. thyme
¼ tsp. black pepper
4 individual pizza bases or pieces of pita bread
1 can tomato or pizza sauce

Preheat the oven to 425°F. Combine the vegetables, oil, vinegar, thyme and pepper in a large baking dish and toss to mix well. Bake, stirring occasionally, for 20 minutes or until the vegetables are tender. Set aside. Place pita bread on baking sheets. Spread about 2 Tbsp. of the tomato sauce on each pita then top with the roasted vegetables & cheese. Bake for 10 to 12 minutes.

Makes 4 servings

Stuffed French-Bread Pizza

1 2-foot-long French-bread loaf
2 Tbsp. olive oil
1 pkg. vegan Italian sausage, crumbled
½ pkg. vegan pepperoni, chopped
1 small red bell pepper, seeded and chopped
1 small onion, chopped
2 large garlic cloves, minced
1 pkg. frozen spinach, thawed, squeezed dry, and chopped
Salt and pepper, to taste
1 tub Tofutti plain cream cheese
1 block Italian-style seasoned tofu, crumbled
½ cup grated vegan parmesan
1 block vegan mozzarella, grated
1 tsp. dried oregano
1 tsp. crushed red pepper flakes

Preheat the oven to 425°F. Split the bread lengthwise, hollow each piece out, and cut in half horizontally, making 4 shells for the pizzas. Heat the olive oil in a skillet over a medium-to-high flame and brown the sausage and the vegan pepperoni. Add the red bell pepper, onion, and garlic. Cook for 3 minutes and then add the spinach. Remove from the heat, season with the salt and pepper, and transfer to a bowl. Combine with the Tofutti cream cheese, the seasoned tofu, and the vegan parmesan and mix thoroughly. Spread the mixture into the bread shells. Top each pizza with the vegan mozzarella. Place on a cookie sheet and bake for 10 to 12 minutes or until the cheese melts and the bread is lightly crisp. Remove from the oven. Top with the oregano and the hot pepper flakes and serve.

Makes 4 French-bread pizzas

Tofu and Japanese Eggplant Skewers
With Red Curry Coconut Sauce

For the Sauce:

1 ⅔ cups unsweetened coconut milk
1 Tbsp. cardamom
2 garlic cloves, chopped
2 Tbsp. brown sugar, packed
1 Tbsp. fresh lime juice
1 Tbsp. Thai red curry paste
Salt, to taste

Combine all the ingredients in a small saucepan. Bring to a simmer and cook for 10 minutes. Turn off the heat and steep, covered, for 15 minutes. Strain and reserve the sauce. Adjust the seasonings.

For the Skewers:

1 ½ lbs. extra-firm tofu, cut into ¾-inch dice
1 ½ lbs. Japanese eggplant, skin on and cut into ¾-inch dice
¾ lb. whole shiitake mushrooms
1 lb. red peppers, cut into ¾-inch dice
15 soaked bamboo skewers
½ cup vegetable oil
2 Tbsp. toasted sesame oil
Salt and pepper, to taste

Thread the tofu, eggplant, mushrooms, and peppers on soaked skewers. Brush with the oils and season with the salt and pepper. Grill on each side for 5 minutes, or until the vegetables are softened and browned. Serve with the prepared sauce.

Makes 15 skewers

Indian Style Rolled Tacos

2 tsp. olive oil
¾ cup red onion, minced
2 cloves garlic, minced
4 Tbsp. chunky peanut butter
3 yams, cooked, peeled, and mashed
2 cups black beans, cooked and slightly mashed
2 tsp. cumin
1 tsp. curry
¼ tsp. red pepper
1 tsp. cinnamon
12 6-inch flour tortillas
2 Tbsp. vegetable margarine
2 Tbsp. maple syrup
½ cup green onion, chopped
4 Tbsp. cilantro

1 cup of your favorite salsa Heat the oil in a skillet and sauté the onion and garlic for 2 minutes, or until tender. Add the peanut butter, yams, and black beans. Add the cumin, red pepper, and cinnamon. Cook until heated. To assemble, spread the bean mixture over the tortillas, tuck in the ends, and roll. Melt the vegetable margarine and combine with the maple syrup. Baste the tacos in the margarine mixture. Bake the tacos at 400°F for 4 minutes on each side, or until golden brown. Serve with the green onion, cilantro, and your favorite salsa.

Makes 6 servings

Thai-Style Stir-Fry

3 Tbsp. peanut oil
1 cup 2-inch tofu strips
1 cup green beans, sliced into 2-inch strips
1 cup 2-inch carrot strips
1 cup chopped broccoli
1 cup red pepper sliced
1 cup green pepper sliced
½ cup chopped baby corn
3-4 green chilies, sliced
1 Tbsp. chopped garlic
2 stems lemon grass, sliced into strips
6-7 fresh lime leaves
1 tsp. lime juice
Salt, to taste

Heat the oil in a large pan or wok. Stir-fry the tofu over high heat until the edges are light brown. Remove from the pan and set aside. In the same pan, stir fry the vegetables for 4 minutes or until slightly softened. Add the stir-fried tofu, chilies, garlic, lemon grass, and lime leaves and stir for 3 minutes. Add the lime juice and the salt and stir. Serve warm.

Makes 4 servings

Sesame Bok Choy and Mushroom Stir-Fry

2 cloves garlic, minced
8 oz. button mushrooms, quartered
8 oz. fresh shiitake mushrooms, stems removed and sliced
1 Tbsp. low-sodium soy sauce
1 large bok choy cut into ½-inch pieces
½ cup chopped green onions
¼ cup vegetable stock
2 tsp. ginger root, minced
2 Tbsp. toasted sesame seeds
1 tsp. dark sesame oil

In a large nonstick skillet or wok, sauté the garlic and mushrooms in soy sauce for 3 minutes. Add the bok choy and green onions and stir-fry for another 3 minutes. Stir in the vegetable stock and ginger. Reduce heat and simmer for 5 minutes. Sprinkle the sesame seeds and sesame oil, if desired, over the mixture before serving.

Makes 6 servings

Vegetables & Sides

...Risotto with Sun-Dried Tomatoes....

Stuffed Pumpkin

2 small pumpkins or baby pumpkins
4 Tbsp. vegan butter blend
3 onions, minced
3 celery stalks, diced
3 carrots, diced
1 tsp. salt
½ cup water
3 cups brown rice, cooked
1 tsp. rosemary
½ tsp rubbed sage
½ cup roasted pumpkin seeds

Cut off the tops and scoop out the seeds and membranes.* Set aside. Preheat the oven to 350°F. Heat 1 Tbsp. of the oil in a large skillet. Sauté the onions until lightly browned. Add the celery and carrots and sauté for a few minutes. Add the salt and water. Simmer for 10 minutes. Add the rice, rosemary, sage, and roasted pumpkin seeds. Fill the pumpkin shells with the rice mixture. Place in a baking dish and cover with foil. Bake for 1 ½ hours, or until the pumpkin sides are soft enough to eat but are not collapsing.

*Note: If you are unable to find packaged, roasted pumpkin seeds at the store, clean the seeds from these pumpkins and rinse in a colander. Brush 1 tsp. of vegetable oil on a cookie sheet and spread the seeds in a single layer. Bake at 350 degrees for 10 minutes, or until lightly browned.

Makes 6 servings

Grilled Garlic-Herb Corn

1 cup margarine, softened
Salt and pepper, to taste
1 Tbsp. minced parsley
1 Tbsp. minced basil
1 Tbsp. minced chives
6 garlic cloves, crushed
6 ears corn, husked
Add cayenne for a kick

Combine the margarine, salt, pepper, parsley, basil, chives, and garlic. Cover and refrigerate for 2 hours. Spread the herbed margarine over the corn, covering completely. Wrap in aluminum foil and grill for 15 to 20 minutes, turning often, until cooked thoroughly.

Makes 6 servings

Grilled Red Potatoes

Extra-virgin olive oil
8-10 baby red potatoes, quartered
1 onion, sliced
1 Tbsp. minced garlic
Salt and pepper, to taste

Stack 2 approximately 2-foot-long pieces of aluminum foil on top of each other. Spread a layer of olive oil in the center and top with the potatoes, onions, and garlic. Season with the salt and pepper. Drizzle with olive oil until lightly coated. Fold over the aluminum foil to create a packet. Double fold the edges to ensure that the potatoes stay sealed. Cook on a grill for 20 minutes, flipping occasionally, until potatoes are lightly crispy.

Makes 4 to 6 servings

Spinach-and-Vegetable Dim Sum

1 cup cooked spinach
1 cup cooked broccoli
1 cup cooked Shanghai cabbage or watercress
2 Tbsp. finely chopped tree ear mushrooms
2 Tbsp. diced shitake mushrooms
¾ cup diced cooked carrots
¾ cup vegetarian burger crumbs
2 Tbsp. sesame oil
¼ cup canola oil
1 tsp. sea salt
1 tsp. white pepper
1 pkg. spinach wonton wrappers

Mix all the ingredients, except for the spinach wonton wrappers, together in a large bowl. Spoon into the center of the wrappers. Gather the corners and seal to create a bundle. Steam for 10 minutes and serve.

Makes 4 to 6 servings

Risotto With Sun-Dried Tomatoes

3 cups vegan chicken broth
3 cups water
1 onion, finely diced
2 cloves garlic, minced
3 Tbsp. olive oil
1 cup rice
¼ tsp. freshly ground red pepper
½ cup oil-packed sun dried tomatoes, drained and chopped
¼ cup fresh basil, chopped
1 Tbsp. fresh parsley, chopped
3 Tbsp. vegan parmesan "cheese"

Mix broth with water and set aside. In a large saucepan over medium heat, sauté the onion and garlic in the olive oil until translucent. Add the rice and sauté for 3 to 4 minutes, stirring constantly, until the rice crackles and starts to brown. Add 1 cup of the broth/water mixture and the pepper, stirring constantly until all moisture is absorbed—about 5 minutes. Add the sun dried tomatoes, basil, and parsley. Continue adding 1 cup of liquid at a time, stirring constantly until all moisture is absorbed before adding the next cup. When the final cup of liquid is absorbed, the rice should be slightly firm but tender, not crunchy. Stir in the nondairy parmesan "cheese" and serve. Makes 4 servings

Roasted Brussels Sprouts

16-20 Brussels sprouts
Salt, to taste
¼ tsp. red pepper
3 Tbsp. balsamic vinegar (optional)
4 Tbsp. extra virgin olive oil

Wash and trim the base of the sprouts and remove the dead discolored leaves. Cut them in half, arrange in a baking dish, and set aside. Mix the salt, pepper, and vinegar in a bowl and whisk until the salt is dissolved. Slowly beat in the olive oil and pour the mixture over the Brussels sprouts. Bake in a preheated oven for about 25 minutes at 375. Turn after about 15 minutes to ensure even cooking. They are done when they look brown and glazed. Reheat and serve hot.

Makes 4 servings

Vegan Red Beans and Rice

1 cup onions, diced
1 cup celery, diced
1 cup green pepper, diced
3 Tbsp. olive oil
48oz. can diced tomatoes with juice
48oz. can red beans with liquid
½ cup garlic, diced
3 bay leaves
3 Tbsp. thyme
1 tsp. cayenne pepper
2 Tbsp. paprika
1 Tbsp. onion powder
¾ cup vegan margarine
¾ cup all-purpose flour
½ cup vegetable stock
Salt, to taste
Dash liquid smoke, to taste

Sauté the onions, celery, and peppers over low heat until translucent but not brown. Add the tomatoes and red beans (with liquid). Stir in the garlic and seasonings, except for the salt and liquid smoke. Simmer over low heat until tender. Make a medium-brown roux: Melt the margarine in a saucepan over medium heat. Whisk in the flour. Turn the heat to high and whisk constantly until the roux is the color of caramel sauce. Remove from heat and allow to cool. Stir the simmering beans and slowly add the roux a little bit at a time until you've reached the desired consistency. Add the salt and the liquid smoke to taste and stir. Serve over rice.

Makes 5 large servings

Tomato Rockefeller

½ cup onion, diced
3 Tbsp. olive oil
2 Tbsp. garlic, minced
5 cups spinach, roughly chopped
¼ cup freshly chopped basil
2 Tbsp. freshly chopped parsley
½ tsp. sea salt
¼ tsp. paprika
⅛ tsp. freshly red pepper
⅛ tsp. ground nutmeg
4 large tomatoes
2 Tbsp. breadcrumbs

Sauté the onion in the olive oil for 3 minutes to soften. Add the garlic and sauté an additional 1 minute. Add the spinach, fresh herbs, salt, paprika, pepper, and nutmeg, and sauté an additional 2 minutes or until spinach wilts. Remove the skillet from the heat. Carefully remove the stems from the tomatoes, then cut them in half crosswise, remove the seeds while keeping the tomatoes halves intact. Place the tomato halves, cut-side up, in a casserole dish. Divide the spinach mixture evenly among the tomato halves and then sprinkle the breadcrumbs over the top. Bake at 375 degrees for 15 minutes or until the breadcrumbs are lightly browned.

Serves 6

Mushroom & Spinach Triple Grain Pilaf

6 cups vegetable broth, divided
1 cup pearl barley, rinsed and drained
¾ cup millet, rinsed and drained
¾ cup quinoa, rinsed and drained
1 tsp. salt
1 ½ cups green onions, thinly sliced
1 cup onion, diced
2 Tbsp. olive oil
12 oz. baby bella mushrooms, sliced
1 ½ Tbsp. garlic, minced
2 Tbsp. sesame seeds
2 Tbsp. toasted sesame oil
5 cups spinach, roughly chopped
⅓ cup freshly chopped parsley
2 Tbsp. freshly chopped thyme
2 Tbsp. tamari
½ tsp. freshly ground black pepper
⅛ tsp. cayenne pepper

In a saucepan, place 3 cups vegetable stock and pearl barley, and bring to a boil. Reduce heat to low, cover, and simmer for 45-50 minutes or until barley is tender. Remove from heat, drain off any excess water, and set aside. Meanwhile, in another saucepan, place the remaining vegetable stock, millet, quinoa, and salt, and bring to a boil. Reduce heat to low, cover, and simmer for 15 minutes or until the grains are tender and most of the liquid has been absorbed. Drain off excess water, leave the grains in the saucepan covered, and let sit for 5 minutes to allow the grains to steam. In a large skillet, sauté the green onions and onion in olive oil for 5 minutes to soften. Add the mushrooms and sauté an additional 3 minutes. Add the garlic and sesame seeds, and sauté an additional 2-3 minutes or until the vegetables are tender. Add the toasted sesame oil and all three cooked grains to the skillet, and sauté for 3 minutes to heat through. Add the remaining ingredients and continue to sauté until the spinach wilts. Taste and adjust the seasonings, as needed. Transfer the pilaf to a large bowl for service.

Serves 8-10

Sautéed Green Apples and Leeks

This is a German favorite.
2 large leeks, white parts only, rinsed
2 Tbsp. vegan margarine
2 large Granny Smith apples, cored and thinly sliced
Salt and pepper, to taste

Cut the leeks in half lengthwise and trim the bottoms, leaving a little of the root end intact so that they stay together. Wash well and dry. Cut into thin strips, about 2 inches long. In a medium skillet over medium heat, melt 1 Tbsp of the margarine. Add the leeks and cook until soft, about 3 minutes. Remove from the pan and set aside. In the same pan, melt the remaining 1 Tbsp. of margarine and add the apple slices. Turn the heat to high and cook until the apples are lightly browned and softened, about 3 minutes. Return the leeks to the pan and toss together to combine. Serve immediately.

Makes 4 servings

Sweet Potato Twice Baked

6 large sweet potatoes, washed well (do not peel)
3 Tbsp. maple syrup
2 Tbsp. orange juice
2 tsp. ginger, minced
1 t. salt

Using a fork, pierce the skins of the sweet potatoes in several places. Place an oven-proof rack on a cookie sheet and place the sweet potatoes on the rack. Bake at 400 degrees for 60-75 minutes or until soft. Remove the cookie sheet from the oven and leave the sweet potatoes on the rack to cool. When they are cool enough to handle, cut each one in half lengthwise. Using a spoon, carefully scoop out the cooked flesh into a food processor, leaving the skin intact to form a shell, and set skins aside. Add the maple syrup, orange juice, ginger, cinnamon, and salt to the food processor, and puree for 2-3 minutes or until very smooth and creamy.

Lightly oil large cookie sheet or baking pan, and place the reserved sweet potato skins in the pan. Refill the skins with the puree mixture, and then swirl the top of each filled skin decoratively with the back of a spoon. Bake at 350 degrees for 15-20 minutes or until heated through. Using a spatula, carefully transfer the halves to a large platter for service. Serve one Twice-Baked Sweet Potato half per person. Serves 12

Zucchini Boats

3 to 5 medium zucchini
1 medium onion, chopped
1 Tbsp. olive oil
1 lb burger crumbles
3 Tbsp. nutritional yeast flakes
1 tsp. garlic salt
½ tsp. oregano
16 oz tomato sauce

Slice the zucchini lengthwise, scoop out the pulp, chop, and set aside. In a nonstick pan, brown the onion in olive oil. Combine the onion, burger crumbles, zucchini pulp, nutritional yeast, garlic salt, and oregano in a large bowl. Fill the boats with the crumble mixture. Pour the tomato sauce over the zucchini boats, overflowing into the pan. Cover with tin foil and bake for 20 minutes at 375°F. Remove the foil and bake for another 15 minutes. Serve hot.

Makes 6 servings

Mexican Rice

2 large onions
3 cloves garlic, minced
¼ cup olive oil
½ tsp. ground coriander seed
1 tsp. light chili powder
1 tsp. cumin
¼ tsp. ground cloves
¼ tsp. freshly ground black pepper
2 cups long-grain white rice
3 cups puréed tomatoes
2 tsp. salt
1 ½ cups boiling water

Peel and coarsely chop the onions, mince the garlic, and sauté them both in the olive oil until the onions are a golden color. Add the chili powder, cumin, coriander, cloves, and pepper, stir, and then add the rice. Continue sautéing the mixture, stirring often, until the rice is coated. Add the puréed tomatoes, salt, and boiling water. Stir the mixture once, then cover and simmer the rice over low heat for another 25 minutes. All the liquid should be absorbed.

Makes 8 servings

Vegan Dumplings #3

1 Quart vegetable stock
2 cups unbleached flour
2 tsp. baking powder
1 tsp. dry mustard
¼ tsp.. cayenne
1 tsp. salt
3 Tbsp. vegan margarine
¼ cup soy milk
Garnishes: freshly chopped parsley and non-hy-drogenated margarine

In a large pot, place the vegetable stock, and bring to a boil. Meanwhile, in a small bowl, place the flour, baking powder, pepper, mustard and salt, and stir well to combine. Using a pastry blender or a fork, cut in the margarine until mixture resembles a coarse meal. Stir in the soy milk, mixing to form a manageable dough. Transfer the dough to a floured work surface and roll out to ⅛-inch thickness. Cut the dough into 1 x 1-inch strips and toss the strips with a little additional flour to prevent them from sticking together.

Carefully drop the cut dumplings in the boiling stock, cover, and cook for 10 minutes without lifting the lid. Remove the dumplings from the vegetable stock with a slotted spoon and transfer them to a large bowl. Save the vegetable stock for making soups. Sprinkle the dumplings with a little chopped parsley and Spectrum Spread (1-2 T. or to taste), and toss gently. Serve as a side dish, or as an accompaniment to soups and stews, or they can also be cooked directly in a simmering soup or stew for added flavor. Serves 6-8

Pine Nut & Squash Risotto

5 cups vegetable stock, divided
⅓ cup pine nuts
3 Tbsp. olive oil, divided
1 cup shallot, finely diced
1 Tbsp. garlic, minced
1 lb. butternut squash, peeled, deseeded, and cut into 1-inch cubes
3 Tbsp. freshly chopped sage
1 ½ cups Arborio rice
½ cup white grape juice
2 Tbsp. Bragg Liquid Aminos
½ tsp. salt
¼ tsp. red pepper
⅓ cup soy parmesan cheese
2 Tbsp. freshly chopped parsley

In a medium saucepan, place the vegetable stock, and bring it to a simmer over low heat. In a large saucepan, place the pine nuts and 2 Tbsp. olive oil, and cook over low heat for 2-3 minutes or until pine nuts are lightly browned. Using a slotted spoon, remove the pine nuts from the olive oil, place them in a small bowl, and set aside. In the hot olive oil, sauté the shallot and garlic for 3-4 minutes or until soft. Add the cubed winter squash and sage, and sauté for 3 minutes or until the sage is fragrant. Add 1 ½ cups of the hot vegetable stock to the saucepan, cover, reduce the heat to low, simmer for 20-25 minutes or until the winter squash is tender. Remove the lid and allow any remaining liquid in the pan to cook off.

Add the remaining 1 Tbsp. olive oil and Arborio rice to the saucepan, and sauté for 1 minute to coat the rice with the olive oil. Add the reserved toasted pine nuts, white grape juice, Bragg Liquid Aminos, salt and pepper, and cook, stirring frequently, until all of the liquid is absorbed. Add ½ cups of the hot vegetable stock to the saucepan, and continue to cook, stirring frequently, until all of the stock is absorbed. Continue adding the vegetable stock in ½ cups increments, while stirring frequently, until all of the stock is incorporated and the rice is creamy and slightly al dente. Add the soy parmesan cheese and parsley, and stir well to combine. Taste and adjust the seasonings as necessary. Individual servings can be topped with additional soy parmesan cheese, if desired. Serves 6

Sausage Stuffing

12 pieces white bread
1 yellow onion fine diced
3 celery stalks find diced
1 Tbsp. olive oil
12oz soy sausage
2 cups vegan chicken stock
1 packet poultry-seasoning herbs (fresh sage, rosemary, thyme, etc.)

Preheat the oven to 350° F. Lightly grease a cookie sheet. Tear the bread into bite-size pieces and spread on the cookie sheet. Bake until toasted. Transfer to a large bowl. In a sauté pan over medium heat, sauté the onion and celery for 1 minute. Break the "sausage" into bite-sized pieces and add to the pan, stirring often. Add 2 Tbsp. of the stock and let simmer for a few minutes, until the "sausage" is slightly browned. Add the spices and cook for a couple of minutes. Pour over the breadcrumbs and mix thoroughly. Add enough of the remaining stock to dampen the bread. Spread into a 9- x 13-inch baking pan and place several sprigs of fresh thyme on top. Cover with foil and bake at 350°F for 15 minutes. Makes 6 to 8 servings

Potato Pancakes

1 large baking potato
½ medium onion
Egg substitute equivalent of 1 egg
1 Tbsp. chopped parsley
1 Tbsp. flour
1 Tbsp. bread crumbs
¼ tsp. thyme
1 lemon, juiced
Salt and pepper, to taste
olive oil
⅓ cup applesauce

In a food processor, grate the potato and onion. Squeeze out the excess liquid and place the dry potato-onion mixture in a bowl. Combine with the egg substitute, parsley, flour, bread crumbs, thyme, lemon juice, salt, and pepper. Mix together. Warm ½ cup of oil on high heat in a skillet. Add ½ cup of the potato mixture to the oil and flatten into a thick pancake. Turn the heat down to medium. Cook for 5 minutes on each side, or until golden brown. Do the same with the rest of the potato mixture. Top with the applesauce.

Makes 3 servings

Cheesy Scalloped Potatoes

2 Tbsp. dried minced onion
1 garlic clove, crushed
1 Tbsp. minced parsley
2 tsp. salt
red pepper, to taste
8 medium potatoes, sliced
8 oz. vegan cream cheese, cubed

Lightly grease a slow cooker. In a small bowl, combine the onion, garlic, parsley, salt, and pepper. Layer ¼ of the sliced potatoes on the bottom of the slow cooker. Sprinkle with ¼ of the seasoning and top with ⅓ of the vegan cream cheese cubes. Repeat the layers, ending with the seasonings. Cover and cook on high for 3 to 4 hours, or until the potatoes are tender. During the last half hour of cooking, stir the potatoes.

Makes 4 to 6 servings

Pumpkin Dumplings

1 cup canned solid-pack pumpkin
Egg Replacer, equivalent to 2 eggs
1 tsp. sea salt
1 tsp. dry mustard
¼ tsp. grated nutmeg
¼ tsp. baking powder
1 cup all-purpose flour
6 Tbsp. vegan margarine
½ cup vegan parmesan cheese

Bring a large pot of salted water to a boil. Place the pumpkin, egg replacer, salt, nutmeg, mustard, and baking powder in a large bowl and whisk to blend. Mix in the flour (the dough will be soft). Dip a ½-teaspoon measuring spoon into the boiling water to moisten. Drop generous ½-teaspoonfuls of the dough into the water. Repeat until all the dough has been used. Boil the dumplings for approximately 10 minutes, or until cooked through. Using a slotted spoon, transfer to a colander and drain. Melt the vegan margarine in a large heavy skillet over medium heat. Add the dumplings. Sauté for approximately 8 minutes, or until beginning to brown. Transfer to a bowl and sprinkle with the vegan cheese before serving.

Makes 4 servings

Orange-Scented Sweet Potatoes

6 baked sweet potatoes
5 Tbsp. orange juice
1 tsp. grated orange rind
1 tsp. grated lemon rind
1 tsp. grated fresh ginger root
Pinch of ground nutmeg
2 ½ Tbsp. maple syrup
¼ tsp. salt or to taste

Lightly toasted, chopped pecans for garnish
Preheat the oven to 350 degrees. Peel the sweet potatoes and put the flesh into a food processor, along with the remaining ingredients. Process until smooth. Bake the purée in a casserole dish until heated through, about 15 minutes. Garnish with the pecans and serve hot.

Makes 6 servings

Boston Baked Beans

These slightly sweet beans with veggie bacon are great with your veggie dogs and veggie burgers.

1 lb. dry Great Northern beans
Water sufficient to cover the beans
1 Tbsp. baking soda
½ tsp. salt
1 cup molasses
1 tsp. dry mustard
1 tsp. vegan Worcestershire sauce
1 cup firmly packed brown sugar
1 Tbsp. vegetable broth powder
½ lb. vegan ham, roughly chopped
1 large white onion, diced
¼ cup diced red bell pepper

Place the beans in a large kettle. Cover with the water and sprinkle with the baking soda. Bring to a boil. Cover and cook for 45 minutes, or until just tender. Combine the salt, molasses, dry mustard, vegan Worcestershire sauce, brown sugar, and vegetable broth powder. Crock pot cook, adding water if needed. Mix well. Cook on low heat for 10 hours, or until the beans are tender.

Makes 6 to 8 servings

Twice-Baked Potatoes #2

4 baking potatoes
½ cup nondairy sour cream
3 Tbsp. margarine, divided
2 Tbsp. faux bacon bits
¼ cup vegan parmesan
2-3 Tbsp. chives, chopped
Salt and pepper, to taste
Paprika

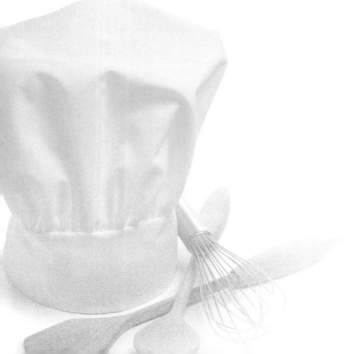

Preheat the oven to 450°F. Poke a few holes in each potato, or wrap in aluminum foil, and bake for 45 minutes, or until tender. Allow them to cool slightly, lightly roll potatoes to soften insides, cut open the top of each, then scoop out most of the insides of the potatoes, leaving about ¼ inch in the shell. Put the scooped-out potato into a bowl, add the nondairy sour cream and 2 Tbsp. of the margarine, and mash or whip until smooth and fluffy. Stir in the faux bacon bits, nondairy parmesan, chives, salt, and pepper and then fill each potato shell with this mixture. Place the potatoes on a baking sheet. Melt the remaining 1 Tbsp. of margarine and brush or drizzle it over the top of each potato. Sprinkle the potatoes with paprika, and cook them in the oven for another 10 minutes until the tops are browned.

Makes 4 servings

Chicken Stuffed Baked Potato

4 large baking potatoes
4 tsp. olive oil
4 Tbsp. taco or fajita seasoning
1 Tbsp. olive oil
1 bell pepper, fine chopped
½ cup chopped white onion
2 cups chopped vegan chicken
4oz. can diced green chilies
1 cup salsa

Preheat the oven to 375°F. Poke several holes into the potatoes. Coat with the olive oil and sprinkle with the seasoning. Bake for 45 minutes, or until soft on the inside and lightly crisp on the outside. Meanwhile, heat the olive oil in a sauté pan over medium heat. Add the bell pepper and onion. Sauté until tender. Add the remaining ingredients and cook until heated through. Slice the potatoes and stuff with the filling.

Makes 4 servings

Roasted Corn With Chipotle Mayonnaise

For the Corn:
⅓ cup chipotle salsa (see recipe)
⅔ cup vegan mayonnaise
8 ears corn with the husks intact
Sea salt, to taste

Preheat the oven to 375°F. Mix the salsa (see recipe below) with vegan mayo. Add salt to taste. Fold down each layer of the corn husks. Remove the silks and use a brush to coat each corn cob with the mixture. Replace the husks and place on a baking sheet. Cover with foil and cook for 35 to 40 minutes. Remove the foil and cook uncovered 5 to 10 minutes more. Fold down the husks and season with salt to taste.

For the Chipotle Salsa:
1 lb. tomatoes, cut in half
1 chipotle chili
½ small white onion, minced
1 Tbsp. olive oil
3 cloves garlic, minced
1 tsp. cumin
1 tsp. sea salt, or to taste

Broil the tomatoes until slightly blackened (leave skin on). Heat the chili on a griddle until soft, about 30 to 40 seconds. Open and remove the seeds. Simmer in water for 10 minutes. Drain. Blend the chili with the tomatoes until smooth. Sauté the onion in oil. Add the garlic and cumin and cook until soft. Add tomato mixture. Cook until thick and dark, stirring occasionally. Add salt to taste and water to the desired consistency.

Makes 8 servings

Pumpkin Risotto

1 cup diced sweet yellow onion
2 cups arborio rice
1 cup apple cider
¼ cup slivered almonds
2 cups vegetable stock combined with 2 cups water
1 cup pumpkin
1 tsp. grated ginger
1 tsp. grated nutmeg
4 sprigs mint, sliced
1 Tbsp. olive oil
Salt, to taste
Pepper, to taste

Dice the onion and sauté over medium heat until translucent. Lower the heat to low or medium-low and add the rice. Cook for approximately 2 or 3 minutes, then slowly add the apple cider, stirring until absorbed. Add the almonds so that they will soften as you develop the risotto. Slowly add in small amounts of the vegetable stock-and-water mixture, setting aside 1 cup. Stir continuously until the liquid is absorbed.

(This can take 30 minutes, and it's important to stir the rice often to develop the gluten and create the creaminess of a proper risotto.) When 3 cups of the vegetable stock-and-water mixture have been added, add the pumpkin, ginger, and nutmeg, then slowly stir in the remaining cup of the stock mixture until absorbed into the rice. Stir in the mint and let cook for an additional 2 minutes. Remove from the heat and add the olive oil, salt, and pepper before serving. The best way I've found to serve this is in pumpkin bowls. For individual servings, get a mini pumpkin for each person you will serve, and slice the tops off at a diagonal angle. Hollow out the insides and roast the shells for about 10 minutes at 350°F. Fill with the risotto, and top with a sprig of mint. The other way to serve this is best for a party where people will be serving themselves. Use a medium-size pumpkin and follow the same technique described above. This is a pretty, unusual holiday dish that's guaranteed to please.

Makes 4 servings

Sage Potatoes

6 medium potatoes
2 Tbsp. olive oil
2 Tbsp. ground sage
2 tsp. paprika
Salt and pepper, to taste
Use baked potatoes that have been refrigerated over night.

Cut, with the skin on, into small chunks. In a large skillet, heat the oil over medium-high heat. Place the potatoes in the pan and sprinkle with the sage, paprika, salt, and pepper. Stir until well blended. Continue frying, turning the potatoes occasionally, until the desired crispness is achieved, about 20 minutes.

Makes 6 servings.

DESSERTS & BAKING

..............Sugar Free Carrot Cake......

Raisin Bran Muffins

2 ½ cups wheat bran
1 ½ cups whole wheat flour
2 tsp. baking soda
2 tsp. baking powder
1 tsp. cinnamon
½ tsp. ground ginger
½ t. sea salt
¼ tsp. ground nutmeg
1 ½ cups apple juice
¼ cup blackstrap molasses
2 Tbsp. sunflower oil, plus additional
for oiling pan
¾ cup carrots, shredded
½ cup raisins

Lightly oil a muffin pan and set aside. In a large bowl, place the wheat bran, whole wheat flour, baking soda, baking powder, cinnamon, ginger, salt, and nutmeg, and combine. In a small bowl, place the apple juice, molasses, and sunflower oil, and whisk well. Add the wet ingredients to the dry ingredients and stir well. Add the remaining ingredients and gently fold them into the muffin batter. Fill each of the prepared muffin cups ¾ full with the batter. Bake at 350 degrees for 25-30 minutes or until an inserted toothpick comes out clean. Remove the muffin tin from the oven and allow the muffins to cool before removing them from the muffin tin. Yield: 1 Dozen

Pumpkin Pie

¾ lb. silken tofu
1 16-oz. can pumpkin
1 ½ tsp. cinnamon
½ tsp. allspice
1 tsp. nutmeg
1 tsp. salt
⅓ cup oil
1 tsp. vanilla
1 cup light brown sugar
1 ½ Tbsp. molasses
1 unbaked 9-inch pastry crust

Preheat oven to 350° degrees. Blend ingredients except the pastry crust in a blender until smooth and creamy. Pour this mixture into the unbaked pastry shell. Bake for 1 hour. Chill and serve.

Makes 1 pie

Strawberry Mouse

3 cups strawberries, tops removed
2 - 12.3 oz. pkgs. tofu, extra firm
½ cup brown rice syrup or maple syrup
½ tsp. almond extract
½ tsp. vanilla

In a food processor, puree the strawberries until smooth. If desired, pass the strawberry puree through a sieve to remove the seeds, and then return the puree to the food processor. Add the remaining ingredients and process for 1-2 minutes or until light and creamy. Transfer the strawberry mousse to a glass bowl, cover, and chill for 1 hour. Top individual servings with additional sliced strawberries or other fruit, granola, or nuts.

Yield: 4 Cups

Almond Chocolate Chip Cherry Cookies

½ cup soy milk, water, or apple juice
½ cup maple syrup
½ cup safflower oil
1 Tbsp. vanilla
1 Tbsp. almond extract
1 cup unbleached flour
1 cup whole wheat pastry flour
1 tsp. baking powder
½ tsp. baking soda
¼ tsp. salt
¾ cup vegan chocolate chips
⅓ cup dried cherries
⅓ cup sliced almonds

Whisk together the soy milk, maple syrup, oil, vanilla, and almond extract, and set aside. In a large bowl, place both types of flour, baking powder, baking soda, and salt, and stir well. Add the wet ingredients to the dry ingredients and stir well. Fold the remaining ingredients into the cookie dough. Lightly oil two non-stick cookie sheets. Drop the dough by teaspoonfuls, spacing them 2 inches apart, onto the prepared sheets. Bake at 350 degrees for 10-15 minutes, or until cookies are set and lightly browned on the bottom and around the edges. Allow the cookies to cool on the cookie sheets for a few minutes before transferring to a rack to cool completely. Repeat the baking procedure for the remaining cookie dough. Store the cookies in an air-tight container. Yield: 24-30 cookies

Vegan Rosemary-Cheese Biscuits

2 cups flour
1 Tbsp. baking powder
½ tsp. salt
¼ cup vegan margarine
1 cup soy milk
½ cup vegan cheddar cheese
1 Tbsp. crushed dried rosemary
1 Tbsp. dried basil
1 Tbsp. sage
1 Tbsp. thyme

Preheat the oven to 375°F. Put all the ingredients in a bowl and mix by hand. Drop by tablespoonful onto a greased baking sheet. Cook for 10 to 12 minutes.

Makes approximately 1 dozen

Corn Muffins

1 ½ tsp. Egg Replacer
3 Tbsp. water
1 cup corn meal
1 cup unbleached flour
1 Tbsp. baking powder
½ tsp. salt
4 T. unbleached cane sugar
1 cup soy milk
¼ cup corn oil
Pinch red pepper flakes
Pinch Parsley

In a small bowl, whisk egg replacer and water together until frothy, and set aside. In a large bowl, combine corn meal, flour, baking powder, salt, and sugar, pepper flakes and parsley. Add soy milk and corn oil to the egg replacer mixture and whisk well. Add wet ingredients to the dry ingredients, stirring just enough to mix. Fill greased muffin pans ½ to ⅔ full. Bake at 425 degrees for 15 – 20 minutes or until lightly browned. Yield: 12 muffins.

Chocolate Chip Hazelnut Biscotti

1 cup hazelnuts
2 cups whole wheat pastry flour
1 cup unbleached flour
1 Tbsp. baking powder
½ tsp. salt
⅔ cup maple syrup
⅔ cup safflower oil, divided
1 ½ tsp. vanilla
1 tsp. almond extract
2 cups vegan chocolate chips

Bake hazelnuts on a cookie sheet at 325 degrees for 15 minutes or until fragrant. Remove the hazelnuts from the oven and increase the temperature of the oven to 350 degrees. Allow the hazelnuts to cool slightly, place them on a towel, enclose them with the towel, and rub the hazelnuts with the towel to loosen their skin. Transfer the hazelnuts to a cutting board, roughly chop them, and set aside. In a large bowl, stir together both types of flour, baking powder, and salt. In a small bowl, place the maple syrup, ½ cups safflower oil, vanilla, and almond extract, and whisk well to combine. Add the wet ingredients to the dry ingredients and stir well to combine. Fold the chopped hazelnuts into the dough.

Line two cookie sheets with parchment paper and set one aside for later use. On the remaining cookie sheet, shape the dough into two logs that are 2 ½ inches wide. Bake at 350 degrees for 30 minutes or until golden brown and feel firm and dry. Remove them from the oven and allow them to cool slightly. When cool enough to handle, transfer the logs to a cutting board, and cut diagonally into ½-inch thick slices. Divide the slices between the two cookie sheets, standing them upright, and spacing them an inch apart. Bake an additional 15-20 minutes or until dry and crisp. Allow cookies to cool.

While the cookies are cooling, prepare the chocolate coating. In the top of a double boiler, place the chocolate chips and remaining 2 Tbsp. safflower oil, and cook over low heat until chocolate chips have melted. Stir the melted chocolate chip mixture until smooth. Dip one of the cut sides of each biscotti into the melted chocolate and then place them chocolate side up on a rack. When you have finished coating all of the biscotti, place the rack in the refrigerator to allow the chocolate coating to harden fully. Store the biscotti in an airtight container.

Yield: 20-24 biscotti

Homemade Pasta Dough

2 cups unbleached flour
4 oz. silken tofu
2 Tbsp. extra virgin olive oil
2 Tbsp. cold water
½ tsp. salt

Combine all the ingredients in a free-standing mixer with a dough hook attachment. Set the mixer on its lowest setting and stir until a ball of dough forms. Continue mixing for another 5 minutes. Cover with plastic wrap and let rest in the refrigerator for 20 minutes.

Roll out by hand or using a machine and shape as desired.

Makes 3 to 4 servings

Chocolate Tofu Cheesecake

Filling:
10 oz. vegan chocolate chips
2 - 12.3 oz. pack Tofu, extra firm
¼ cup maple syrup
1 Tbsp. vanilla
⅛ tsp. salt

Crust:
1 ½ cups graham cracker crumbs
3 Tbsp. carob powder
1 Tbsp. unbleached cane sugar
½ cup safflower oil

Begin by pressing the tofu. In a large colander, place a natural unbleached coffee filter, place the two blocks of tofu in the coffee filter, cover the tofu blocks with another coffee filter, place a plate on the top of the coffee filter, and then a heavy can or weight on top of the plate. Place the colander over a bowl, then place the entire set-up in the refrigerator, and leave to drain for several hours or overnight. Melt the chocolate chips in the microwave or over a double boiler. In a food processor or blender, combine the pressed tofu, melted chocolate chips, and remaining filling ingredients, and puree until smooth.

In a small bowl, combine graham cracker crumbs, cocoa, and sugar, stirring until well mixed. Drizzle in safflower oil, and using your fingers, mix until thoroughly combined. Firmly press into the bottom of a greased 9-inch springform pan and set aside. Pour filling over top of crust and bake at 325 degrees for 45 minutes. Allow to cool, and chill, preferably overnight, or for several hours. Garnish with fresh fruit or sliced almonds, if desired.

Yield: One 9-inch cheesecake, or 12 pieces

Super Soy Biscuits

2 ¼ cups unbleached flour
¾ cup soy flour
3 T. unbleached sugar
2 T. baking powder
¾ tsp. cream of tartar
½ tsp. salt
¾ cup vegan margarine
1 cup soy milk

Sift together both types of flour, sugar, baking powder, cream of tartar, and salt. Using a pastry blender or a fork, cut the margarine into the dry ingredients until the mixture resembles coarse crumbs. Drizzle the soy milk over the mixture and stir lightly to form a dough. Transfer the dough to a lightly floured work surface. Using your hands, gather the dough into a ball and knead gently a few times. Roll out or pat the dough with your hands to a ¾-inch thickness. Using a round 2 ½-inch cookie cutter or knife, cut the dough into 12 biscuits. Transfer the cut biscuits to a non-stick cookie sheet and space them 1-inch apart. Bake the biscuits at 425 degrees for 10-12 minutes or until lightly browned.

Yield: 1 Dozen

Cinnamon and Raisin Bread Pudding

6 cups stale bread of choice, cut into 1-inch cubes
⅓ cup raisins
2 ½ cups soy milk
1 cup apple juice
½ cup maple syrup
1 Tbsp. vanilla
2 tsp. cinnamon
1 tsp. salt
¼ tsp. nutmeg

Lightly oil a 8 x 12-inch casserole dish. Place the bread cubes in the casserole dish and scatter the raisins over the bread cubes. In a small bowl, whisk together the remaining ingredients, and pour over the top of the bread cubes. Bake at 350 degrees for 40-45 minutes or until golden brown on top. Remove from the oven and allow to sit for 10 minutes before cutting into servings. Serve warm, cold, or at room temperature, and can be served plain, topped with tofu whipped topping, or with a scoop of non-dairy ice cream or sorbet. * Note: you can substitute other dried fruit for the raisins, and add up to ¼ cups rum or other liqueur of choice to the wet mixture before pouring it over the bread cubes.

Yield: One 8x12-inch pan or 6-8 servings

Raspberry Tofu Cream Topping

12 oz tofu, extra firm
¼ cup raspberry juice
2 Tbsp. sugar
1 Tbsp. safflower oil

In a food processor or blender, combine all of the ingredients and puree for several minutes until smooth and creamy. Transfer to a glass or plastic container and store in the refrigerator. Serve as a topping for fruit, pies, and desserts.

Yield: 1 ½ cups

Cranberry Bread

2 ½ cups unbleached flour
¾ cup unbleached cane sugar
1 T. baking powder
3 T. water
1 Tbsp. Ener-G Egg Replacer
⅓ cup Spectrum Spread non-hydrogenated margarine
1 cup soy milk
1 Tbsp. vanilla
1 cup fresh or frozen cranberries, roughly chopped
1 Tbsp. lemon zest

Lightly oil a 9x5x3-inch loaf pan and set aside. In a bowl, place the flour, sugar, and baking powder, stir well to combine, and set aside. In another bowl, place the water and egg replacer, and whisk vigorously for 1 minute or until very frothy (almost like beaten egg whites). Add the Spectrum Spread and whisk until smooth. Add the soy milk and vanilla, and whisk well to combine. Add the dry ingredients to the wet ingredients and stir until just moistened. Add the remaining ingredients and stir until just combined.
Pour the batter into the prepared pan. Bake at 350 degrees for 60-70 minutes or until an inserted toothpick comes out clean. Place the loaf pan on a rack to cool for 10 minutes, remove the loaf from the pan, and cool completely before slicing or storing. Store wrapped in plastic wrap or aluminum foil.

Yield: One 9x5x3-inch loaf

Banana Pops

3 cups bananas, cut up
⅔ cup soy milk
3 Tbsp. carob powder
3 Tbsp. turbinado sugar
1 Tbsp. vanilla

In a food processor, combine all of the ingredients, and process for 2-3 minutes to form a smooth puree. Fill 8 (3 oz.) frozen ice pop molds with the mixture and insert sticks. Freeze for at least 6 hours or overnight. Allow them to sit at room temperature for several minutes for easy removal from molds. Serve immediately or wrap individually and store in the freezer.

*Note: Mini paper cups and wooden sticks or spoons can be substituted for the frozen ice pop molds.   Yield: 8

Almond Granola

4 cups rolled oats
1 cup raw wheat germ
1 cup sliced almonds
1 cup raw sunflower seeds
½ cup flax seeds
1 ½ tsp. cinnamon
1 ½ tsp. ground ginger
¼ tsp. ground nutmeg
½ cup apple juice
¼ cup blackstrap molasses
¼ cup safflower oil
1 Tbsp. vanilla
1 Tbsp. almond extract

Line two cookie sheets with pieces of parchment paper and set aside. In a large bowl, place the rolled oats, wheat germ, almonds, sunflower seeds, flax seeds, cinnamon, ginger, and nutmeg, and toss well to combine. In a small bowl, place the remaining ingredients, and stir well to combine. Pour the wet ingredients over the dry ingredients and stir well to thoroughly moisten the dry ingredients. Transfer the granola mixture to the prepared cookie sheets, evenly dividing it between the two pans, spreading it to form a single layer. Bake at 300 degrees for 20 minutes.

Remove the cookie sheets from the oven, stir the granola mixture, spread it out to form a single layer again, and bake the granola mixture an additional 20 minutes. Remove the cookie sheets from the oven, stir the granola mixture, spread it out to form a single layer again, switch the placement of the cookie sheets on the racks, and bake the granola mixture an additional 20 minutes. Repeat the stirring and spreading procedure, as needed, until the granola mixture is dry and golden brown. Remove the cookie sheets from the oven and set the granola aside to cool completely. Transfer the granola to an airtight container and can store at room temperature for 4-6 weeks.

Yield: 2 Quarts

Dried Fruit and Coconut Candies

1 cup dried apricots
1 cup dates, pitted
1 cup raisins
1 cup walnuts
1 cup shredded coconut
4 Tbsp. lemon or orange juice
shredded coconut, for coating candies

In a food processor, place the apricots, dates, raisins, and walnuts, and process for 1 minute to finely chop the ingredients. Add the coconut and lemon juice and process an additional 1-2 minutes or until mixture comes together to form a ball. Place some shredded coconut on a plate and set aside. Dampen hands with water, roll the mixture into 1-inch balls, and then roll the shaped balls in the shredded coconut. Store the candies in an airtight container.

Yield: 20-24 pieces

✳ Oatmeal Raisin Cookies ✓

1 ¾ cups whole wheat pastry flour
1 ⅔ cups rolled oats
1 ¼ cups oat bran
2 tsp. cinnamon
½ tsp. baking powder
¼ tsp. nutmeg
1 cup apple of choice, peeled, sliced, and divided
½ cup frozen apple juice concentrate, thawed
½ cup maple syrup
⅓ cup safflower oil
1 Tbsp. vanilla
½ tsp. almond extract
⅔ cup raisins
½ cup chopped walnuts

In a large bowl, place the flour, oats, oat bran, cinnamon, baking powder, and nutmeg, and stir well to combine. Finely dice ½ cups of the sliced apples and set aside. Place the remaining sliced apples in a blender or food processor, and puree. Add the apple juice concentrate, maple syrup, oil, vanilla, and almond extract, and blend for 1 minute. Add the apple puree mixture to the dry ingredients and stir well to combine. Fold in the reserved apple, raisins, and walnuts. Drop the batter by rounded tablespoonfuls on to two non-stick cookie sheets. Bake at 350 degrees for 12-15 minutes or until lightly browned around the edges and on the bottom. Allow the cookies to cool on the cookie sheets for 3 minutes before transferring them to a rack to cool completely. Store in an airtight container.

Yield: 2 Dozen

Apple Walnut Bread

2 cups applesauce
½ cup apple juice
½ cup maple syrup
¼ cup safflower oil
1 Tbsp. vanilla
1 cup unbleached flour
1 cup whole wheat flour
4 tsp. baking powder
1 Tbsp. cinnamon
½ tsp. salt
½ cup chopped walnuts

Grease a 9x5x3-inch loaf pan and set aside. In a large bowl, combine the applesauce, apple juice, maple syrup, oil, and vanilla, and whisk well to combine. In another bowl, sift together both types of flour, baking powder, cinnamon, and salt. Add the dry ingredients to the wet ingredients and stir well. Fold in the chopped walnuts. Pour the batter into the prepared loaf pan. Bake at 350 degrees for 55-60 minutes or until golden brown and an inserted toothpick comes out clean. Place the loaf pan on a rack and allow cooling for 15 minutes. Remove the loaf of bread from the pan and allow cooling completely on a rack before slicing. Wrap the loaf in aluminum foil and store in the refrigerator or freeze the loaf for later use.

Yield: One 9x5x3-inch loaf

Apricot Date Bar Cookies

Filling:

1 ½ cups dried apricots, diced
1 cup dates, pitted and diced
¾ cup orange juice
⅓ cup Sugar
3 Tbsp. orange zest
⅛ tsp. ground ginger

Base:

¾ cup sugar
¾ cup Vegan margarine
1 ¾ cups unbleached flour
1 tsp. salt
½ tsp. baking soda
½ tsp. cinnamon
1 ½ cups rolled oats

Lightly oil a 9 x 13-inch baking pan and set aside. Begin by preparing the filling: in a small saucepan, combine all of the filling ingredients and cook over low heat, stirring occasionally until thickened, about 7-10 minutes. Remove the pan from the heat and set aside to cool completely. To prepare the base for the bar cookies: in a medium bowl, stir together the Sugar and margarine. Add the flour, salt, baking soda, and cinnamon, and stir until well blended. Add the oats and stir well to combine.

Transfer half of the base mixture to the prepared pan. Using your hands, press firmly to flatten the mixture to cover the bottom of the pan. Spread the cooled apricot-date filling over the base, then sprinkle the remaining base mixture over the filling, and pat it down lightly. Bake at 400 degrees for 25-30 minutes or until lightly browned. Allow to cool for 5 minutes. While still warm cut into 36 equal bars and remove them from the pan. Store in an airtight container.

Yield: One 9 x 13-inch pan or 36 bars

Nectarine & Mango Sorbet

1 ½ cups water
½ cup unbleached cane sugar
1 ½ lbs. nectarines, peeled, pitted, and sliced
1 mango, peeled, pitted, and sliced
1 cup orange juice
2 Tbsp. lemon juice

In a saucepan, place the water and sugar, and bring to a boil. Stir mixture to help dissolve the sugar, reduce the heat to low, and simmer for 5 minutes. Remove mixture from the heat and allow cooling for 10 minutes. In a blender or food processor, place the nectarines, mango, and cooled sugar mixture, and process for 1 minute.

Add the orange juice and lemon juice and puree the mixture until very smooth. Pour the mixture into an ice cream maker and freeze according to the manufacturer's instructions.

If you do not have an ice cream maker, place sorbet mixture in a plastic container, cover, and chill for 3-4 hours or until partially frozen. Process sorbet mixture in a blender or food processor. Return the mixture to the plastic container, cover, and freeze 3 additional hours. Repeat the processing procedure, transfer back to the plastic container, cover, and freeze until solid. Serve as an accompaniment to cakes, pies, desserts, or as a refresher.

Honeydew and Mint Sorbet

6 cups honeydew melon, cut into1-inch cubes
¾ cup frozen apple juice concentrate, thawed
¼ cup freshly chopped mint
¼ cup lime juice

In a food processor or blender, in batches if necessary, combine all of the ingredients and puree until smooth. Taste and add more apple juice concentrate or mint if needed to balance the ripeness of the melon. If you have an ice cream maker, freeze the mixture according to the manufacturer's instructions, or transfer the mixture to an airtight container, place in the freezer, and freeze for several hours or until firm. One hour before serving, process the mixture in the food processor again, return it to the airtight container, and refreeze until firm. Serve in chilled glasses and, if desired, add a garnish of fresh fruit and a sprig of mint.

Serves 8

Coconut Fudge Packs

2 Tbsp. water
1 Tbsp. Egg Replacer
½ cup unbleached cane sugar, plus additional for rolling out dough
¼ cup carbo powder
¾ cup vegan margarine, divided
¼ cup shredded coconut
¼ cup walnuts, finely chopped
1 Tbsp. vanilla, divided
1 ½ cups unbleached flour
¼ tsp. salt
3 Tbsp. Soy milk

In a small bowl, combine the 2 Tbsp. water and egg replacer, and whisk vigorously for 1 minute or until very frothy (almost like beaten egg whites). Add the sugar, carob powder, ¼ cups margarine, coconut, chopped nuts, and 1 tsp. vanilla. Stir well to combine, and set aside. In a medium bowl, stir together the flour and salt. Using a pastry blender or a fork, cut in the remaining margarine into the flour mixture, and work it until the mixture resembles coarse crumbs. Drizzle the flour mixture with the remaining 3 Tbsp. water and 2 tsp. vanilla, and mix well to form a soft dough.

Lightly oil two non-stick cookie sheets and set aside. Sprinkle a work surface with a little sugar to prevent the dough from sticking. On the sugared surface, roll out the dough to $1/16$-inch thickness, and cut it into 2 ½-inch squares.

To assemble each of the pastries: place 1 teaspoonful of the filling in the center of each square, fold each of the corners of the square up to the center, and gently press them together to partially seal in the filling. Using a spatula, transfer the pastries to the prepared cookie sheets with the sealed seam-side up.

Bake at 350 degrees for 15-20 minutes or until set and lightly browned. Allow the pastries to cool on the cookie sheets for several minutes before transferring them to a rack to cool completely. When completely cooled, transfer to an airtight container for storage, and place waxed paper between the layers of pastries.

Yield: 28-30 pieces

Non-Dairy Vanilla Ice Cream

2 cups water
3 Tbsp. agar-agar flakes
2 - 12.3 oz. pkgs. tofu, extra firm
1 ½ cups soy milk
1 cup unbleached cane sugar
2 Tbsp. vanilla
½ tsp. salt

In a small saucepan, place the water and agar-agar flakes, and simmer for 5 minutes to thoroughly dissolve the agar-agar flakes. Meanwhile, in a food processor, process the tofu to a smooth puree. Add the agar-agar mixture and the remaining ingredients, and process for 1-2 minutes or until very smooth and creamy. If you have an ice cream maker, transfer the mixture to the ice cream maker and freeze according to the manufacturer's instructions. Or, pour the mixture into a large shallow pan, and place it in the freezer. Stir the mixture every hour or so to give it a smooth texture. When completely frozen, remove it from the freezer, and allow it to sit at room temperature for 15 minutes. Transfer the mixture to a food processor, process until smooth, and transfer the mixture to an airtight container. Return it to the freezer and freeze until solid. Serve as an accompaniment to cakes, pies, desserts, or as a refresher.

*Variation: if you don't mind the extra fat, adding a few tablespoons of a mild vegetable oil to the mixture before freezing will result in a rich and creamy texture. Feel free to experiment with the recipe by adding additional flavorings, or chopped fruit or nuts.

Yield: 1 ½ Quarts

Vegan Chocolate Chip Ice Cream

¾ cup unbleached cane sugar
½ cup water
2 cups vegan chocolate chips
2 - 12.3 oz. pkgs. tofu, extra firm
1 ½ cups soy milk
2 Tbsp. vanilla
½ tsp. salt

In a small saucepan, place the sugar and water, and simmer for 5 minutes to thoroughly dissolve the sugar and form a syrupy consistency. Remove the saucepan from the heat and set aside. Place the chocolate chips in the top of a double boiler (over simmering water) and allow the chocolate chips to melt. Meanwhile, in a food processor, process the tofu to a smooth puree. Add the sugar-syrup mixture, melted chocolate chips, and the remaining ingredients, and process for 1-2 minutes or until very smooth and creamy. Taste and add additional sweetener or vanilla, if desired. If you have an ice cream maker, transfer the mixture to the ice cream maker and freeze according to the manufacturer's instructions. Or, pour the mixture into a large shallow pan and place it in the freezer. Stir the mixture every hour or so to give it a smooth texture. When completely frozen, remove it from the freezer and allow it to sit at room temperature for 15 minutes. Transfer the mixture to a food processor, process until smooth, and transfer the mixture to an airtight container. Return it to the freezer and freeze until solid. Serve as an accompaniment to cakes, pies, desserts, or as a refresher.

Feel free to experiment with the recipe by adding additional flavorings, or chopped fruit or nuts.

Yield: 1 ½ Quarts

Lemon Frosting

½ cup soy margarine, softened
3 oz. tofu cream cheese, softened
2 Tbsp. soy milk
4 cups Vegan Powdered Sugar
1 Tbsp. lemon juice
1 tbsp. lemon zest

Using an electric mixer or in a large bowl with a hand held mixer, place the soy margarine, tofu cream cheese, and soy milk, and cream them together. Add half of the sugar, and beat well to combine. Add the remaining ingredients and continue to beat the mixture until light and fluffy.

Yield: 3 Cups or enough for two 9-inch layers or a 9x13-inch cake

Tofu Cream Cheese Frosting

8 oz. tofu cream cheese, softened
⅓ cup vegan margarine
3 cups Vegan Powdered Sugar
2 tsp. vanilla
1 tsp. almond extract

Using an electric mixer or in a large bowl with a hand held mixer, place the tofu cream cheese, and cream them together. Add the sugar, vanilla, and almond extract, and continue to beat the mixture until light and fluffy.

Yield: 2 ½ cups or enough for two 9-inch layers or a 9x13-inch cake

Sugar Free Carrot Cake ✓

2 cups whole wheat flour
1 tsp. baking powder
1 tsp. baking soda
¼ tsp. salt
1 ¼ cups water
1 ¼ cups dates, chopped
1 cup raisins
2 tsp. cinnamon
1 tsp. ground ginger
½ tsp. ground cloves
½ tsp. ground nutmeg
½ cup carrot, shredded
½ cup chopped walnuts
⅓ cup frozen orange juice concentrate, thawed

Lightly oil a 9-inch springform pan and set aside. In a small bowl, sift together the flour, baking powder, baking soda, and salt, and set aside. In a small saucepan, combine the water, dates, raisins, cinnamon, ginger, cloves, and nutmeg. Bring to a boil, reduce heat, and simmer for 5 minutes. In a large bowl, place the shredded carrots, pour the hot liquid mixture over the top, and allow cooling completely. Add the walnuts and orange juice concentrate to the carrot mixture and blend well. Add the dry ingredients to the wet ingredients and stir well to combine. Pour the batter into the prepared springform pan. Bake at 375 degrees for 45 minutes or until an inserted toothpick comes out clean. Serve plain or frost with Tofu Cream Cheese Frosting, or Lemon Frosting, or Vanilla Butter Cream Frosting, or other frosting of choice.

Yield: One 9-inch cake

Vanilla White Cake

1 ⅓ cups unbleached cane sugar
½ cup vegan margarine
3 cups unbleached flour
1 Tbsp. baking powder
½ tsp. salt
2 cups soy milk
1 Tbsp. vanilla
2 tsp. almond extract

Lightly oil a 9x13-inch pan and set aside. Using an electric mixer or in a large bowl with a hand held mixer, place the sugar and Spectrum Spread, and cream together until light and fluffy. In another bowl, sift together the flour, baking powder and salt. Add dry ingredients into the creamed mixture, alternating with the soy milk, and continuing to beat the mixture well between each addition. Add the vanilla and almond extract and beat the mixture an additional 2 minutes at medium speed. Pour the batter into the prepared pan. Bake at 350 degrees for 30 minutes or until an inserted toothpick comes out clean. Serve plain or frost with Vanilla Butter Cream Frosting or any of its variations, or Lemon Frosting, or other frosting of choice.
*Note: For a marble variation, reserve ¾ cups of the batter and add an additional ⅓ cups unbleached sugar, ¼ cups margarine, and ¼ cups cocoa. Pour the vanilla batter into the prepared pan. Drop the chocolate batter by spoonfuls on top of the vanilla batter, and use a knife to make a swirl pattern.

Yield: One 9x13-inch cake

Wheat Free Sugar Free Cut Out Cookies

½ cup brown rice syrup
⅓ cup safflower oil
2 Tbsp. vanilla
1 tsp. almond extract
1 ½ cups barley or spelt flour
½ cup arrowroot
1 tsp. baking powder
½ tsp. salt

Line two cookie sheets with parchment paper or non-stick baking liners and set aside. In a small bowl, place the brown rice syrup, oil, vanilla, and almond extract, and whisk well. In a medium bowl, place the flour, arrowroot, baking powder, and salt, and stir well. Add the wet ingredients to the dry ingredients and stir until well blended. Gather the dough into a ball. Sprinkle a large piece of waxed paper with a little additional flour, place the dough on the floured waxed paper, and place an additional piece of waxed paper on top. Using a rolling pin, carefully roll out the dough to a ¼-inch thickness. Remove the top sheet of waxed paper and cut into desired shapes with cookie cutters. Using a spatula, carefully transfer the cut-outs to the prepared cookie sheets. The cookies can be left plain, or before baking, sprinkle with any toppings on top of the cookies, and gently press with your fingers to help the toppings stick to the dough.
Bake at 350 degrees for 8-10 minutes or until lightly browned on the bottom and around the edges. Allow the cookies to cool on the cookie sheets for a few minutes before transferring them to a rack to cool completely. Repeat the rolling, topping, and baking procedure with the remaining cookie dough. When all of the cookies are cooled completely, store them in an airtight container with waxed paper between the layers.

Yield: 24-30 cut out cookies

Almond Berry Pie

For Pie Crust:
1 ½ cups sliced almonds
¾ cup sunflower seeds
2 cups dates, pitted
½ cup dried banana chips
1 tsp. cardamom
1 tsp. cinnamon

For Berry Filling:
2 ½ cups blueberries
1 cup strawberries
⅓ cup dates, pitted
¼ tsp. cardamom
¼ tsp. cinnamon

Garnishes:
fresh blueberries
sliced strawberries
sliced almonds

Begin by preparing the pie crust. In a food processor, place the almonds and sunflower seeds, and process for 2-3 minutes to form a fine meal. Add the remaining pie crust ingredients, and process for 5 additional minutes or until the mixture comes together. Transfer the mixture to a 9-inch pie pan. Using your hands, press the mixture evenly over the bottom and up the sides of the pie pan. Place in the refrigerator and allow chilling for 20-30 minutes or until firm. Place all of the filling ingredients in the food processor and process for 1-2 minutes to form a smooth puree. Pour the filling into the chilled pie crust. Place the pie in the refrigerator and chill for 30-45 minutes or until filling is set and slightly firm. Score the top of the pie into 8 pieces and decorate each piece of pie with a few fresh berries and sliced almonds.

Yield: One 9-inch pie or 8 pieces

Mint Chocolate Chip Cake

½ cup soy milk
½ cup tofu, extra firm
1 cup water
1 ⅔ cups unbleached cane sugar
1 ½ cups unbleached flour
¾ cup soy flour
¾ cup carob powder
1 ½ tsp. baking powder
1 ¼ tsp. baking soda
1 tsp. salt
½ cup applesauce
2 tsp. vanilla
½ tsp. peppermint oil
1 cup vegan chocolate chips

Lightly oil two 8-inch round cake pans and set aside. In a food processor or blender, place the soy milk and tofu, and blend for 1 minute. Add the water and blend an additional 30 seconds. In a medium bowl, sift together the sugar, flour, soy flour, baking powder, baking soda, and salt. Add the dry ingredients to the food processor and blend for 1 minute. Add the applesauce, vanilla, and peppermint, and blend an additional 30 seconds or more to combine. Add the chocolate chips and pulse 2-3 times to incorporate. Divide the batter evenly between the two pans. Bake at 350 degrees for 30-35 minutes or until an inserted toothpick comes out clean. Place the cakes on a rack to cool for 5 minutes. Then invert the layers on to a rack, remove the pans, and allow cooling completely before frosting.

Yield: Two 8-inch layers

Cranberry Pecan Tartlets

1 cup vegan margarine
4 oz. tofu cream cheese
1 ½ cups unbleached flour
½ cup pecans, finely chopped
1 - 12 oz. pkg. fresh or frozen cranberries
½ cup dark corn syrup
⅓ cup Sucanat
¼ cup apple juice
⅓ cup unbleached cane sugar
3 Tbsp. cornstarch
¼ tsp. salt
2 tsp. vanilla
1 tsp. almond extract
1 cup pecan halves

In a small bowl, cream together ¾ cups margarine and tofu cream cheese until light and fluffy. Add the flour and chopped pecans, and thoroughly mix to form a soft dough. Shape the dough into a ball, cover, and chill for 45 minutes. Lightly oil eight 4-inch tart pans and set aside. When the dough has thoroughly chilled, transfer it to a work surface and knead it a bit with your hands to soften it up. Divide it into 8 equal pieces and place one piece of dough in each of the prepared tart pans. For each tart pan: place one piece of dough, and using your fingers, press the dough to cover the bottom and sides of the tart pan. Repeat the procedure for the remaining tart pans. Place the tart pans on two cookie sheets and chill them while preparing the filling.

In a saucepan, place the cranberries, dark corn syrup, Sucanat, apple juice, and remaining ¼ cups margarine, and bring to a boil. Reduce heat to low and simmer for 3-4 minutes or until the skins of the cranberries begin to pop. In a small bowl, stir together the sugar, cornstarch, and salt. Add the cornstarch mixture to the saucepan, stir well to combine, and continue to simmer the mixture for 3-4 additional minutes or until thickened. Remove the pan from the heat and stir in the vanilla and almond extract. Remove the prepared tart shells from the refrigerator. Pour approximately ¼ cups of the cranberry filling into each of the tart shells and decoratively arrange the pecan halves on top of the filling. Bake at 350 degrees for 20-25 minutes or until the pecans and crust are lightly browned. Allow the tartlets to cool in pans completely, loosen edges with a knife, and then carefully remove the tartlets from the pans. Serves 8

Vegan Hot Fudge Sauce

½ cup cocoa or carob powder
2 Tbsp. cornstarch
1 ¼ cups vanilla soy milk
½ cup maple syrup
1 tsp. vanilla

In a bowl, sift together the cocoa and cornstarch. Transfer the cocoa mixture to a small saucepan and whisk ½ cups soy milk into the cocoa mixture. Add the remaining soy milk and maple syrup to saucepan and whisk well. Cook the mixture over medium heat, while whisking constantly for 2-3 minutes or until it forms a thick sauce. Remove the saucepan from the heat and whisk in the vanilla. Serve warm as a topping for cakes, desserts, non-dairy ice cream or as a dipping sauce for fruit. Store in an airtight container, in the refrigerator, and reheat as needed.

Yield: 1 ½ cups

Simple Powdered Sugar

2 cups unbleached cane sugar
½ cup cornstarch

In a blender or food processor, blend sugar and cornstarch for 1 minute. Scrape down the sides and blend an additional 30 seconds.

Simple Powdered Sugar #2

4 cups unbleached cane sugar (or white sugar from sugar beets)
1 cup arrowroot

In a blender or food processor, blend sugar and arrowroot for 1 minute. Scrape down the sides of the blender container and blend an additional 1 minute. Store in an airtight container.

Yield: 4 Cups

Old Fashion Big Loaf

1 medium potato
1 cup warm water
1 - ¼ oz. pkg. active dry yeast
2 T. olive oil, plus additional for oiling bowl and pan
2 cups unbleached flour
1 cup whole wheat flour
½ cup soy flour
2 t. sea salt
1 tsp. sesame seeds
½ tsp. poppy seeds

Begin by baking the potato at 350 degrees for 40-50 minutes or until soft to the touch. Remove the potato from the oven and set aside to cool. When the potato is cool, cut in half, and using a spoon, carefully separate the cooked potato from its skin. Place the cooked potato in a small bowl, mash it well with a fork (should yield 1 cup), and set aside. In a large bowl, place the warm water, yeast, and olive oil. Stir well to dissolve the yeast, and set aside until bubbly, about 10-15 minutes. Add the reserved mashed potato and stir well to combine. Add the unbleached, whole wheat, and soy flours, and salt, and stir well to form a soft dough. Turn the dough out onto a floured work surface and knead, adding additional flour if needed, until smooth and elastic, about 5 minutes. Place a little olive oil in the large bowl, place the dough in the bowl, give it a twist, and turn the ball over to coat the other side. Cover the bowl with a clean towel, place it in a warm place, and leave to rise for 1 hour or until doubled in bulk.

Lightly oil a large cookie sheet or pizza pan, and set aside. When the dough has doubled, transfer it to the oiled pan, and stretch it to form a 10-inch circle. Sprinkle the sesame seeds and poppy seeds over the top. Cover the pan with a clean towel, place in a warm place, and leave to rise for an additional 1 hour or until doubled in bulk. Remove the towel from the pan. Bake the loaf at 425 degrees for 15 minutes or until lightly golden brown. Transfer the loaf to a rack to cool.

Yield: One 10-inch loaf

Vanilla Butter Cream Frosting

½ cup Vegan margarine, softened
¼ cup soy milk
3 cups Vegan Powdered Sugar
2 tsp. vanilla

Using an electric mixer or in a large bowl with a hand held mixer, place the soy margarine and soy milk, and cream them together. Add half of the sugar, and beat well to combine. Add the remaining ingredients and continue to beat the mixture until light and fluffy.

*Note: For a Berry Frosting, add ¼ cups mashed fresh or frozen berries, such as raspberries, strawberries, or blueberries.

For a Chocolate Frosting, add ½ cups carob powder or ⅓ cups melted vegan chocolate chips. You can also stir in chopped nuts, chopped vegan chocolate, shredded coconut, or chopped fruit into the basic Vanilla Butter Cream Frosting recipe to create additional variations.

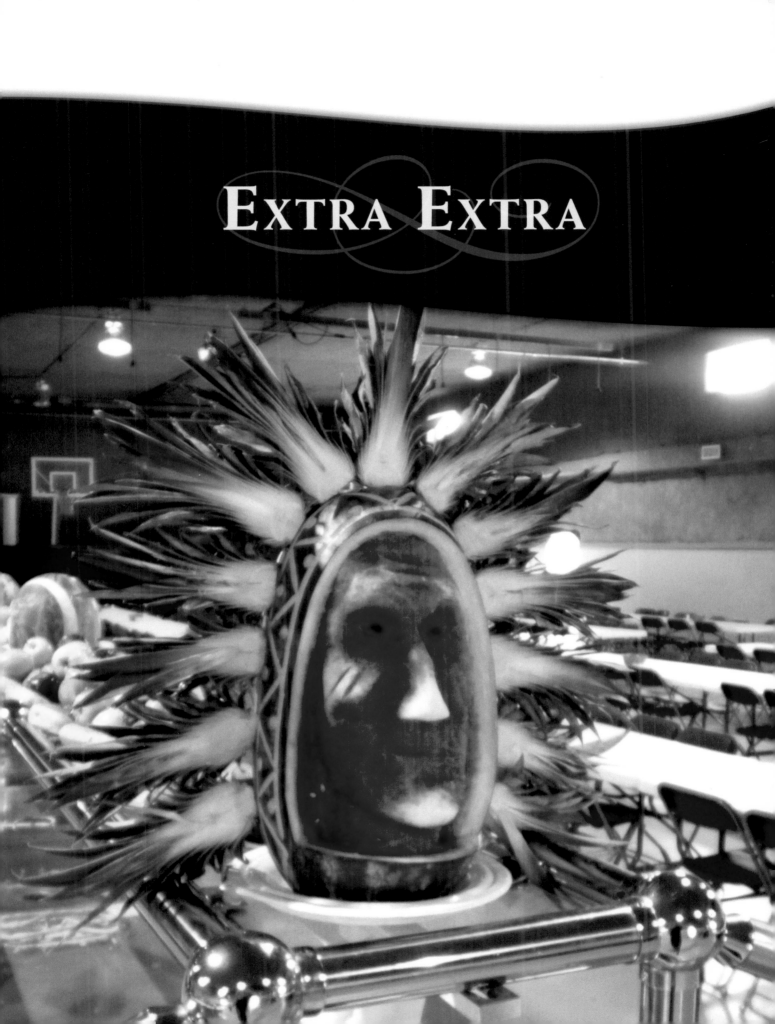

Decorators Frostings

1 cup Vegan Powdered Sugar # 2
1 tsp. vanilla
3 tsp. soy milk

In a small bowl, stir together the Vegan Powdered Sugar # 2 and vanilla. Add soy milk a little at a time, stirring well after each addition to reach spreading consistency. Spread on cookies using a knife, spatula, or a pastry bag. Allow frosting to dry completely before stacking cookies.

*Note: If desired, you can tint the frosting with natural food coloring. Or use fruit juice concentrate (such as raspberry or blueberry) as a replacement for the soy milk in the recipe, for a more natural tint.

Cajun Popcorn

1 cup raw popcorn kernels
2 Tbsp. safflower oil
1 Tbsp. water
1 Tbsp. nutritional yeast flakes
1 Tbsp. Cajun seasoning
¼ tsp. salt

Using a hot air popper or other popcorn popper, pop the popcorn and place it in a large bowl. In a small saucepan, combine the remaining ingredients, and cook over medium heat for 1-2 minutes to blend the flavors. Drizzle the oil mixture over the popcorn and toss well to evenly coat the popcorn. Serve warm.

Serves 6-8

Quick-and-Easy Dry Rub

½ cup paprika
¼ cup brown sugar
3 Tbsp. garlic powder
3 Tbsp. onion powder
1 Tbsp. dried coriander
1 Tbsp. red pepper

Salt to taste
✦ Combine all the ingredients and mix well.

Makes 1 cup

Taco Seasoning

1 Tbsp. chili powder
¼ tsp. garlic powder
¼ tsp. onion powder
¼ tsp. crushed red pepper
¼ tsp. dried oregano
1 tsp. ground cumin
1 tsp. sea salt
1 tsp. pepper

Mix all of the ingredients together until combined.

Vegetarian Sushi

Now you can make this delicacy at home and impress your family and friends with your mastery of Japanese cuisine!

6 cups water
3 cups short-grain brown or white rice
1 small cucumber
1 small zucchini
1 green & red bell pepper
½ onion
2 small carrots
½ lb. fresh spinach
⅔ cup apple cider
6 Tbsp. brown sugar
1 package pre-toasted nori sheets
Prepared wasabi paste

Bring the water to a boil. Add the rice, lower the heat, and simmer for 40 minutes, stirring occasionally. Seed and julienne the cucumber, and julienne the zucchini, bell peppers, onion and carrots. Steam these vegetables, along with the spinach, over boiling water for 5 to 7 minutes. Let cool to room temperature. Mix together the vinegar and brown sugar, and stir until the sugar is dissolved. When the rice is cooked, stir in the vinegar and brown sugar mixture, and cool to room temperature. When the vegetables and rice are cool enough to handle, lay out the first nori sheet. Place a handful of rice in the center of the sheet, moisten your hands with water, and gently but firmly press the rice to the edges of the sheet so that there is a thin layer of rice in a line on the sheet. Spread a bit of wasabi paste on top of the rice, approximately 1 ½ inches from one edge of the nori sheet. Lay vegetable strips parallel to the wasabi in a width of approximately 1 inch along the wasabi line. Carefully wrap the closest edge over the vegetables, then roll the nori delicately but tightly. Seal by moistening the edge of the nori. Once the nori sheet is completely rolled, slice the roll into 6 pieces and arrange on a platter. Repeat with the remaining nori sheets.

Top Tips: If your nori rolls won't stay rolled, try "sealing" the seam with a little brown rice syrup. To make rolling easier and prevent the nori sheets from tearing, use an inexpensive bamboo sushi mat—available in Japanese markets and many health food stores.

Makes 6 rolls

Baked Herb Croutons

4 cups bread of choice, cut into ½-inch cubes
olive oil
½ tsp. dried basil
½ tsp. dried oregano
½ tsp. dried thyme
½ tsp. garlic powder
¼ tsp. onion powder
¼ tsp. paprika

Place the cubes of bread on a non-stick cookie sheet. Drizzle the cubes with olive oil, about 1-2 Tbsp., to taste. In a small bowl, place all of the remaining ingredients, and toss well to combine. Sprinkle the herb mixture over the cubes of bread and toss the cubes to coat them evenly. Spread the cubes of bread to a single layer and bake at 300 degrees for 15 minutes. Remove the cookies sheet from the oven, stir the croutons, and spread them out to a single layer again. Return the cookie sheet to the oven and bake the croutons an additional 10-15 minutes or until lightly browned and crisp. Allow the croutons to cool before using. Store in an air tight container.

Yield: 4 Cups

Whole wheat calzone dough

1 ⅓ cups warm water (110 degrees)
3 Tbsp. olive oil
1 - ¼oz. pkg. active dry yeast
1 ¾ cups whole wheat flour
1 ¾ cups unbleached flour
2 tsp. salt
olive oil

In a food processor, place the warm water, olive oil, and yeast, and process for 30 seconds to combine. Allow the mixture to sit for 10 minutes or until foamy. Add both types of flour and salt, and process an additional 1 minute or until the dough comes together to form a ball. Transfer the dough to a floured work surface and knead the dough for 5-7 minutes or until smooth and elastic. Lightly oil a large bowl with a little olive oil, transfer the ball of dough to the bowl, and roll the dough around the inside of the bowl to thoroughly coat it with the oil. Cover the bowl with a clean towel, place it in a warm place, and leave the dough to rise for 1 hour or until doubled in bulk. After the dough has doubled in size, punch down the dough, and turn it out onto a floured work surface. Knead the dough a few times, place the bowl over the top of the dough, and leave it to rest for 20 minutes. Divide the dough into 8 pieces. Using a rolling pin, roll out each piece of dough to form a 6-inch circle. Place filling of choice on one half of each circle of dough, leaving a ½-inch border around the edge. Brush a little water around the edge of each circle of dough. Fold the dough over to enclose the filling, crimp the edges closed with your fingers, and then fold up the edges a ½-inch to form a decorative border. Transfer the filled calzones to a non-stick cookie sheet and bake at 450 degrees for 20 minutes or until golden brown. Allow the calzones to cool for a few minutes before serving. Can be served warm, cold, or at room temperature.

Yield: 8 Calzones

Black-Bean Dip #2

2 15-oz. cans black beans
1 tsp. chopped garlic
2 Tbsp. chopped fresh cilantro
2 small tomatoes, chopped and divided
2 tsp. fire roasted red bell pepper
1 tsp. cumin
1 tsp chili powder
Juice of 1 lime
2 green onions, chopped
Salt and pepper, to taste

In a food processor, coarsely chop the black beans, garlic, cilantro, chili powder, lime juice and one of the chopped tomatoes. Season with salt and pepper. Transfer to a serving bowl. Top with the red pepper, cumin, onions, and remaining chopped tomato. Chill for 3 hours before serving.

3ABN TODAY Cooking Program Recipes
In The Raw Unedited Format

Spinach & Artichoke Dip

⅓ c vegan cream cheese
¼ c vegan sour cream
8 oz artichoke hearts, drained weight
½ c frozen chopped spinach, drained
1 T chopped Garlic
¼ t pepper
¼ t salt
½ t lemon juice
¼ t Pico de Gallo spice

Blend & Chill for 2 hours

Almond Pate

3 c soaked almonds
2 T tahini
⅔ c lemon juice
¼ c soy sauce
2 t chopped garlic
½ c chopped carrot
1 T flax seed
1 t mesquite seasoning
¼ t salt
¼ t pepper
Optional: 2 cup canned white beans
½ t almond extract

Blend in food processor

Panama Potatoes

3 16 oz cans new potatoes
¼ c Pesto
¼ c jerk spice
¼ cup BBQ spice
½ cup peanut oil

Deep fry or bake new potatoes
Sautee in mixed seasonings

Asian Spring Rolls

1 package rice paper
1 cup shredded green cabbage
1 cup shredded carrots
1 cup shredded shitake mushrooms
½ cup sliver onions
½ cup sliver peppers
¼ cup soy sauce
¼ c olive oil
2 t chopped garlic
1 t ginger
1 T sesame oil
¼ cup peanut oil for frying

Sautee together, in wok if possible
Let cool. And wrap into rice paper
Deep fry, grill or bake in oven

Asparagus & Tofu Teriyaki Castle

3 to 10 packages extra firm tofu
1 bag frozen Asparagus spears
1 bottle teriyaki glaze
Steak seasoning
Vegan beef bouillon cubes of vegan beef stock

Marinate tofu in beef base
Make castle and smother with teriyaki and steak spices
Can also use BBQ and pepper spices
Bake off in oven & top with more glaze

Coconut & Almond Poached Pears

4 under ripe pears, pealed with stems left on
½ cup sugar
¼ c orange juice
2 T lemon juice
2 t grated lemon rind
½ t ginger
¼ cup Almonds Split toasted
1 T Almond extract

Boil
Add pears, Bring to Boil then simmer 25 min. till tender
Top with syrup, almonds and coconut

Vegan Alfredo Sauce

1 package extra firm tofu
2 cups soy milk
1 teaspoon onion powder
1 teaspoon garlic powder
½ teaspoon salt
¼ teaspoon red pepper
¼ teaspoon nutmeg

1 cup vegan rice parmesan cheese
Blend, Heat & Serve

Mark Anthony's Marinara

2 lbs crushed tomato
6 oz paste
½ cup diced peppers
½ cup diced onions (we will keep them out
for you LOL)
2 cloves garlic
2 cups water
2 Tablespoons sugar
1 Tablespoon oregano
1 Tablespoon Basil
½ teaspoon thyme
1 Bay leaf
2 teaspoons salt
1 Tablespoon yellow mustard (secret ingredient)

Simmer for 1 hour

Basil Pesto (Let's do this one)

½ cup salted **soy nuts**
¾ cup olive oil
1 oz basil
1 Tablespoon garlic
¼ teaspoon Kosher salt
¼ cup vegan Parmesan cheese (optional)

Blend

Basil Pesto #2

½ cup pine nuts
1 cup olive oil
3 oz basil
2 Tablespoons garlic
½ teaspoon sea salt
¼ t sugar
¼ cup vegan Parmesan cheese

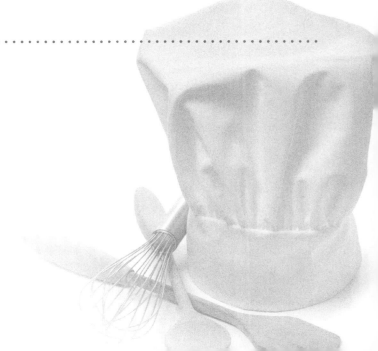

Glossary

Agar-Agar: Sea vegetable that can be used in place of gelatin in many recipes. Available in flakes or bars in Asian markets and health food stores.

Agave Nectar: From the agave plant. Can be used as a replacement for honey. Available in natural food stores.

Arrowroot: Starch that can be used for thickening sauces. Use 1 Tbsp. to thicken 1 cup of liquid. Available in health food stores.

Blackstrap Molasses: Unrefined molasses with a stronger taste than regular molasses. Available in health food stores.

Bragg's Liquid Aminos: Unfermented alternative to soy sauce that can be used to flavor tofu, stir-fries, soups, and pot pies. Available in health food stores.

Brown Rice Syrup: Made from malted brown rice. Can be used in place of sugar, honey, and other sweeteners. Available in health food stores.

Bulgur: Crushed wheat kernels that are typically used in Middle Eastern cuisine. Found in most grocery stores and health food stores.

Carob: Can be used as a replacement for chocolate in baking. Found in health food stores.

Carrageen: Seaweed that can be cooked as a side or used as a gelling agent.

Couscous: A nutty-flavored, quick-cooking grain that can be used in place of rice. Found in grocery stores.

Daikon: A large, white, Japanese radish. Found in specialty markets and Asian markets.

Demerara Sugar: Unrefined cane sugar. Available in most grocery stores and health food stores.

Edamame: A green soybean that can be steamed, sautéed, or tossed into soups. Available in Asian markets and most grocery stores.

Egg Replacer: Can be a powdered replacer, like the one made by Ener-G, or puréed tofu. =

Florida Crystals: A brand of unprocessed sugar. Found in most grocery stores and health food stores.

Galangal: Also known as "Thai ginger." Similar in taste and appearance to ginger. Found in Asian markets.

Garam Masala: Typically used in Indian food. A blend of cumin, black pepper, cloves, fennel, cardamom, dried chili, cinnamon, nutmeg, coriander, and other spices. Found in the ethnic section of most grocery stores.

Herbs de Provence: A mixture of dried herbs from the southern region of France. Normally contains marjoram, savory, fennel, basil, thyme, and lavender.

Hijiki: Dark-green sea vegetable that needs to be rinsed before cooking. Found in Asian markets and health food stores.

Kohlrabi: A root vegetable that is similar in taste to cauliflower. To prepare, boil until tender. Found in many grocery stores and Asian markets.

Kombu: Seaweed that is often used as a flavoring agent in soups, stews, and chilis and for braising tempeh. Found in Asian markets and health food stores.

Kudzu: A starchy powder that can be used to thicken sauces, gravies, and stews. Whisk with cold water until smooth to avoid clumping when adding to a recipe. Found in health food stores. (If you do not have kudzu, cornstarch and arrowroot can be used instead.)

Glossary

Miso: Fermented soybean paste that comes in several varieties. The darker the paste, the stronger and saltier the flavor. Can be used to replace anchovies in Caesar dressing or in a marinade for tofu. Available in Asian markets and health food stores.

Nori: Thin black seaweed typically sold in sheets. Used as a wrapper for sushi. Found in health food stores, Asian markets, or the Asian section of grocery stores.

Nutritional Yeast: Nutty, cheese-like flavored powder. Cannot be replaced with brewer's yeast or active yeast. Found in health food stores.

Pectin: A natural gelling agent found in fruits that can be used to thicken jams and jellies. Found in most grocery stores.

Quinoa: Pronounced "keen-wah." A fast-cooking ancient grain that's loaded with protein. Must be rinsed before cooking. Growing in popularity and can now be found in most grocery stores and in health food stores.

Seitan: Made from wheat gluten. A perfect substitute for meat in any dish. Found in health food stores and Asian markets.

Stevia: A naturally sweet herb with no calories. Much sweeter than sugar. Found in the baking aisle of most grocery stores or in health food stores.

Sucanat: A semi-refined cane sugar that tastes like brown sugar.

Tahini: Made from sesame seeds and also called "sesame butter." Found in the ethnic foods aisle of most grocery stores.

Tamari: True soy sauce. Fermented from soybeans. The wheat-free version of shoyu, another soy sauce. Found in Asian markets and most grocery stores.

Tamarind: A fruity and sour pod from a tropical evergreen. Found in Latin, Asian, and Indian markets.

Tempeh: A cake of pressed soybeans. Found in most grocery stores and health food stores.

Turbinado Sugar: Light brown raw sugar that has been partially refined and washed. Found in more grocery stores.

Umboshi: Tart Japanese plum that is dried and pickled. Found in health food stores and Asian markets.

Index of Recipes

Index of Recipes

Chef Mark Anthony's

New Testimony Book

ORDER NOW!

Mark Anthony is one of the most talented chefs you will ever meet. He has been a chef to some of today's most popular rock stars as well as some of the most powerful people in the world.

Thru his journeys in Las Vegas as both a chef and casino owner, he has experienced the lifestyles of both the filthy rich right down to the homeless and hopeless.

His convictions and desires to transform his life in a different direction than the fast paced life of constant sin found him in a world of churches with lost direction.

It took years of study and visits to well over 200 churches to realize the distortion and the deception happening on a level so large that society in whole is not aware of.

This book is both an inspirational testimony of dedicated conviction to find the real truth as well as an awareness of what's going on in the shadows of a counterfeited light.

Follow him thru this amazing journey in a search for the truth From Sin City To Simplicity.

Mail in check or money order below. Or order online at www.ChefMarkAnthony.com

Mail Orders To: Mark Anthony M.A.L.L. • Box 332 • Ashland, KY 41105-0332

Ship to:_____

Address _____

City, State, Zip _____

Books	Costs	Qty.	Total
From Sin City to Simplicity	$13.00		
Vegan Simplicity Cookbook	$20.00		
Shipping and Handling	$5.00 per book (US)		
		Grand Total	

Make Checks Payable To: Mark Anthony M.A.L.L.

Mark Anthony Lines Limited Website: www.ChefMarkAnthony.com • General email box: spicecreator@yahoo.com